INTRODUCTION TO
KANT'S
ANTHROPOLOGY

SEMIOTEXT(E) FOREIGN AGENTS SERIES
Originally published in French by Librairie Philosophique J. Vrin.
© 2008 Librairie Philosophique J. Vrin
This edition © 2008 Semiotext(e)

Published by Semiotext(e)
2007 Wilshire Blvd., Suite 427, Los Angeles, CA 90057
www.semiotexte.com

Special thanks to José Ruiz-Funes, Dominique Séglard and Robert Dewhurst.

Design: Hedi El Kholti

ISBN-13: 978-1-58435-054-5
Distributed by The MIT Press, Cambridge, Mass. and London, England
Printed in the United States of America

INTRODUCTION TO
KANT'S
ANTHROPOLOGY

Michel Foucault

Edited, with an afterword and critical notes, by Roberto Nigro

Translated by Roberto Nigro and Kate Briggs

\<e\>

Contents

Introduction

Traditionally, complementary theses did not get published. Yet the "translation, with introduction and notes" of *Anthropology from a Pragmatic Point of View* comprised Foucault's complementary thesis. Before it could be submitted to the jury, Foucault had to secure a publisher for *Histoire de la folie*, his main doctoral thesis—such were the rules prior to 1968. The difficulties Foucault encountered have been documented.[1] Moreover, the jury, which included Jean Hyppolite and Maurice de Gandillac, encouraged Foucault to detach his edition of the translation from the commentary, in which they saw the beginnings of an autonomous essay that could be developed further. This, prompting the well-known furor, is what Foucault did: that essay became *Les Mots et les choses*.

The research for the complementary thesis was undertaken between 1959 and 1960 in Hambourg, a town close to Rostock (where Kant's manuscripts are held), where Foucault was the director of the Institut Français. On many occasions, he notes the variations between these manuscripts and the Nicolovius edition. Still, there is no guarantee that this great excavator of archives worked directly with the manuscripts themselves. In the short introduction published with his translation in 1964,[2] Foucault notes that the main variations are in the edition of Kant's work published by the Prussian Academy, which he was using.[3] His other sources can be found in the eleven volumes of the 1922 Cassirer edition that he owned, purchased in Germany.

The "geological depth" of Kant's text—which, over twenty-five years, accompanied the gestation of his critical thinking—is questioned on the basis of the categories of "genesis and structure," in homage to Hyppolite's important work on Hegel's *Phenomenology* (Hyppolite was the supervisor of the thesis). Yet only the beginning and the end of Foucault's text respond to these categories; the heart of the essay appeals to the—Heideggerian—category of repetition. Neither a conclusion to nor a part of Kant's critical enterprise, *Anthropology from a Pragmatic Point of View* establishes a conformity between empirical anthropology—as it stood in the eighteenth century—and critical philosophy. Foucault's research is in fact bound up with what, for him, had been a key question since the 1950s, one already denounced by Husserl: the growing anthropologization of philosophy, from which the Heideggerian thinking that is never cited here, but which is nevertheless very much present, perhaps does not emerge unscathed.

Already in "Connaissance de l'homme et réflexion transcendantale," a course taught at the University of Lille in 1952–3—97 handwritten pages, the oldest philosophical text of Foucault's to have been preserved—Foucault goes back over the destiny of the anthropological theme in nineteenth century philosophy: Kant, Hegel, Feuerbach, Marx, Dilthey, Nietzsche. Of Kant's works, he discusses only the short text of the *Logic*, which G.B. Jäsche published in 1800 with Nicolovius.

From 1952, Foucault was rereading "the great Chinaman of Königsberg [who] was only a great critic"[4] through Nietzsche, and, from 1953, Kant and Nietzsche through Heidegger. The 1954 preface to Binswanger's book[5] and the "Anthropological circle," the last chapter of *Histoire de la folie* attest to this. When, in 1964, following

Georges Canguilhem's advice, he approached Vrin with his translation, he was in a position to announce (in a note) a forthcoming study of the "relationship between critical thinking and anthropological reflection."

It was only in 1963, after having spent a long time contemplating Las Meninas in the Prado, that he had glimpsed the outline of a history of the transition from the age of representation to the age of anthropology. To have published his thesis, which announced this transition but was still ignorant of the method, would have been counterproductive. It was in a recent configuration of knowledge—knowledge of production, of the living and of languages—and not in the destiny of modern philosophy that he now situated the emergence and the likely disappearance of the figure of man that emerged in the eighteenth century as an empirico-transcendental doublet:

> It is probably impossible to give empirical contents transcendental value, or to displace them in the direction of a constituent subjectivity, without giving rise, at least silently, to an anthropology—that is, a mode of thought in which the rightful limitations of acquired knowledge (and consequently of all empirical knowledge) are at the same time the concrete forms of existence, precisely as they are given in that same empirical knowledge.[6]

Why publish this text? And so late? We have just evoked Foucault's reasons for not doing so in 1964. The readers who occasionally consulted the typed manuscript deposited—like all theses—and accessible, hence public, in the Bibliothèque de la Sorbonne (classmark W 1961 (11) 4º) expressed their surprise at its non-publication. For Foucault, then, it was an occasion to bemoan the lack of literary agents in France.

Since his death, the thesis has, in its turn, been the object of a number of theses and translations, many of which are available on the Web.

Typing errors and obscure passages due to the reproduction of Foucault's handwritten corrections have generated much confusion. The practice adopted for the publication of the lectures at the Collège de France has been repeated here: an editorial committee for an authoritative edition at Vrin, a publishing house which Foucault liked to keep company with, where he hoped to publish his translation.

—Daniel Defert, François Ewald, Frédéric Gros
October 2007

Note on the text and translation

What follows is a translation of Michel Foucault's *Introduction à l'"Anthropologie" de Kant*. The *Introduction*, together with his translation of Immanuel Kant's *Anthropologie in pragmatischer Hinsicht* (1798), constituted his secondary doctoral thesis (the principal thesis being *Madness and Civilization*), which was supervised by Jean Hyppolite and submitted to the University of Paris, Sorbonne on May 20, 1961. The translation is based on the copy held at the Bibliothèque de la Sorbonne, University of Paris, and on the recent Vrin edition (Paris, 2008).

The *Introduction* comprises 128 typed pages. Due to smudgings and crossings-out, some of the typed words are illegible. We have indicated in a footnote wherever this introduces an ambiguity with regard to the meaning of text; all other typing errors have simply been corrected. So as to give a sense of the text as a work in progress —a work which Foucault would never prepare for publication—we have translated Foucault's own footnotes, along with a number of handwritten notes and corrections, as they appear in the original. Foucault's footnotes are indicated by asterisks; in square-brackets, we have completed, or sometimes corrected, the bibliographical information he provides; all further editorial notes are numbered.

Foucault was using two editions of the complete works of Kant: the Academy Edition, the first volume of which was published in 1907, but also *Immanuel Kants Werke* (1912–21) edited by Ernst Cassirer.[1] Foucault introduces Kant's *Anthropologie* into his own text in three different ways: by citing directly from the German, by quoting from his own translation (*Anthropologie du point de vue pragmatique* was published by Vrin in 1964)[2] or by silently paraphrasing the German and, when doing so, frequently shifting the emphasis of what is nevertheless still, recognizably, a passage from Kant. These three levels of insertion present the translator with a dilemma. In the name of homogenization, one strategy would be to bring all of the direct citations of Kant in line with the latest English translation. And, to a certain extent, this is what we have done. Kant's *Anthropology* has been translated three times into English, most recently by Robert Louden in 2006. The latest version is not without its own layers of sedimentation: as Louden notes, his translation builds on the two earlier versions, which appeared in 1974 and 1978; it is based on the 1800 edition of a text published two years before, itself the culmination of a project apparently begun in 1772.[3] Wherever Foucault cites directly from the German, we have referred the reader to Louden's translation and to the other volumes in *The Cambridge Edition of the Works of Immanuel Kant*; where Foucault refers to a text which has not been translated into English, we have provided references to the Academy Edition. Foucault frequently cites from his own translation, and when he does so he is evidently referring to the 347 typed pages that, together with the *Introduction*, completed his secondary thesis, and which are also held at the Bibliothèque de la Sorbonne. As one might expect, the pagination of the typed translation differs from that of the Vrin edition. Because the typed copy is effectively inaccessible, we have replaced Foucault's pagination and referred the reader directly to Louden's translation. Since the Cambridge edition of Kant's works also includes the pagination of the Academy Edition, they can also be checked in the English translation.

However, to systematically move from the German directly into English would be to bypass the important detour that Kant's text makes via French—by way of a translation which the examiners of Foucault's secondary thesis deemed to be "correct but not sufficiently subtle."[4] Wherever appropriate, we have drawn on the accepted Kantian lexicon in English; in the name of variance, though, we have also at times sought to register, in English, this passage through French: the circuitous journey that Kant's—for Foucault, irreducibly—German text underwent before reappearing here, at yet another remove from its source. This, after all, is not a translation of Kant's *Anthropologie*, but a translation of Foucault's *Introduction à l'"Anthropologie" de Kant*, and to consistently render, for example, *Mensch* as "human being," would be to disturb the processes of layering and superimposition at work in the original—Foucault writes *homme*.

—Kate Briggs and Roberto Nigro

Introduction to Kant's *Anthropology*

A note in the *Anthropology** indicates that Kant had been delivering his series of lectures for some thirty years before the text was prepared for publication; the lectures in anthropology took up the winter semester, while the summer semester was set aside for physical geography. In fact, that figure is not quite right: by 1756, Kant was already teaching geography; the lectures in anthropology, however, were probably not begun before the winter of 1772–1773.**

The publication of the text we are all familiar with coincided with the end of the semester and with Kant's definitive retirement from teaching. The 1797 edition of *Neues deutsches Merkur* makes a brief mention of the news received from Königsberg: "Kant publishes his *Anthropology* this year. He'd been keeping it under wraps because, of all his courses, anthropology was the most popular. Now that he's no longer teaching, he no longer has any scruples about making the text public."*** Though Kant must have agreed to let his programme of teaching appear on the course prospectus for summer 1797, he had already publicly, if not officially, announced that "due to old age," he "no longer wanted to lecture

---

* *Anthropology*, Preface, p. 6.

** See E. Arnoldt, *Kritische Excurse* (1894), p. 269 ff. [Emil Arnoldt, *Kritische Excurse im Gebiete der Kant-Forschung*, Königsberg, F. Beyer.]

*** Vol. II, p. 82. Quoted by O. Külpe. *Kants Werke* (Academy Edition, VII, p. 354). [See *Der Neue Teutsche Merkur*, Vol. II, 1797. Oswald Külpe edited the *Anthropology* in Volume 7 of the Academy Edition.]

at the University."* The course having been definitively cancelled, he resolved to have the text printed.

We know nothing, or virtually nothing, about the different versions of the text that existed prior to the final draft. After Kant's death, Starke published two collections of his students' and auditors' notes.** Neither of these works, however, can be relied upon; it is hard to have confidence in notes that were published thirty-five years after Kant's death.[1] That being said, the second volume does contain an important element which is not included in the text Kant published: a chapter entitled "*Von der intellectuellen Lust und Unlust.*"[2] According to Starke, the manuscript of this chapter got lost when Kant posted it from Königsberg to the printers at Jena. In fact, there is nothing in the manuscript held in the Rostock library to suggest that a fragment is missing. It is more likely that Kant did not want to make room in the published work for a text which had already been delivered as a lecture. If Starke's first volume has a better claim to our attention, it is because of its specification of the dates: the notes collected in that volume were taken during the winter semester of 1790–1791,[3] which suggests that, on two points relating to the conception and to the very structure of the *Anthropology*, a change must have occurred between the year 1791 and the final draft of the manuscript.***[4]

---

* Quoted by Külpe, (ibid). See E. Arnoldt: *Beiträge zu dem Material der Geschichte von Kants Leben* [Berlin, Bruno Cassirer, 1909.]

** [*Immanuel*] *Kants Anweisung zur Menschen und Weltkenntniss* [*Nach dessen Vorlesungen im Winterhalbjahre 1790–1791*, edited by Friedrich Christian Starke] (Leipzig 1831); [*Immanuel*] *Kants Menschenkunde, oder philosophische Anthropologie* [*Nach handschriftlichen Vorlesungen*, edited by Friedrich Christian Starke] (Leipzig, 1831). [See Friedrich Christian Starke (ed.), *Immanuel Kants Menschenkunde*, Georg Olms, Verlag, Hildesheim—New York, 1976.]

*** See below, p. 70.

Of a text elaborated over a period of twenty-five years, a text which, as Kant's thinking was taken in new directions, must have undergone any number of transformations, we have only one version: the last. The text is given to us already weighed down with sedimentation, having closed over the past in which it took shape. Those twenty-five years—which saw the early researches come to their conclusions, the inception of the critique, the formation of Kantian thought in its tripartite equilibrium, the long-awaited elaboration of a system that could withstand attack from the Leibnitian return, Schulze's scepticism or Fichte's idealism—are all buried deep within the text of the *Anthropology*. And so it goes on, there being no external or reliable criteria available that would offer the means to date any of the layers that give its geological depth.

Still, it would not be uninteresting to discover what fixed coefficient the *Anthropology* shares with the critical enterprise. In 1772, was there already, perhaps even subsisting in the very depths of the *Critique*, a certain concrete image of man which no subsequent philosophical elaboration would substantially alter and which emerges at last, more or less unchanged, in Kant's last published text? Moreover, if that image of man managed to reap the rewards of the critical experience and yet, for all that, still not be subject to any distortion, is this not because it had—if not quite organized and determined that experience—then at least indicated the direction it might take, acting as its secret guide? The *Critique* would therefore have been inclining toward the *Anthropology* from the beginning, and would in some obscure sense be concluded by it. But it is also possible that key elements of the *Anthropology* were modified as the critical enterprise progressed. In which case, if an archaeology of the text were possible, would it not reveal the genesis of a "*homo criticus*," the structure of which would be essentially different from the image of man that went before? Which is to say that, in addition to its particular role as a "propaedeutics" to philosophy, the *Critique* would have also played a constitutive part in the birth and the development of the concrete forms of human existence. Hence there would be a certain *critical* truth to man, a truth born of the critique of the conditions of truth.

But let us not hope for conclusive answers to such unequivocal questions. The text of the *Anthropology* is given to us in its final form. Four series of indications will guide our investigation, all of which are incomplete:

a) The notes or *Reflexionen* pertaining to the anthropology that were collected in the Academy edition with a view to determining their date.* It is worth repeating that only a very few of these fragments are long enough to offer a sense of what the *Anthropology* might have looked like at any given moment, and while the dates are prudently only given as approximations, the organization of the fragments follows the model of the 1798 edition on the assumption that it had gone unchanged since 1772. In such conditions, only changes made to the detail of the text are discernible.

b) The Academy edition of the *Collegentwürfe* divides the notes into two sections: one deals with the years 1770–80, the other with

---

* Prussian Academy Edition, vol. XV. [*Anthropologie*, in *AA*, Bd. XV, 1 and 2, which contains reflections on Baumgarten's *Psychologia Empirica* as well as drafts for the lecture course from the 1770s and 1780s. Some of these fragments are translated in *Notes and Fragments, The Cambridge Edition of the Works of Immanuel Kant*, Cambridge University Press, 2005, chapter 5.]

the period 1780–90.* Despite difficulties similar to those presented by the *Reflections*, comparison of these texts with the 1798 version suggests that there had been a major shift in the meaning of the *Anthropology*, or in the center of gravity of the work (in the *Collegentwürfe*, much more weight is given to the themes of history, citizenship, and cosmopolitanism).⁵

c) Comparison with the texts from the precritical period and with those texts more or less contemporaneous with the final draft of the *Anthropology*. This should enable us to isolate those elements that went absolutely unchanged from the very first lectures to the published version. On the other hand, there can be no doubt that some of the problems with which Kant was preoccupied around the years 1796–1798 had an impact upon the definitive text; in that sense, a number of themes in the 1798 text were recent additions.

d) Comparison with other texts in the field of anthropology of the same period. For instance, certain similarities with Baumgarten's⁶ *Psychologia empirica*,** which Kant had read very early on, give an unequivocal indication of which elements of the *Anthropology* remained constant; on the other hand, other works in the field, along with C.C.E Schmidt's *Empirische Psychologie*,*** reveal which

------

* Ibid. vol. XVI. [In fact, the reference is to *Entwürfe zu dem Colleg über Anthropologie aus den 70er und 80er Jahren*, in *AA*, Bd. XV, 2 (*zweite Hälfte*), pp. 655–899. See *Notes and Fragments*, op. cit, chapter 5.]

** See Kant's notes to *Psychologia empirica*, in vol. 15 of the Academy edition. [*Erläuterungen zur Psychologia empirica in A. G. Baumgartens Metaphysica*, in *AA*, op. cit., vol. XV, 1, pp. 3–54.]

*** Iena, 1790. [Carl Christian Erhard Schmid, (1761–1812), Professor of Philosophy and Theology at Iena, author of *Empirische Psychologie*, Iena, Cröcker, 1791.]

elements must have been added later. But here, once again, we have to be careful: it is often impossible to determine whether Kant was drawing on a book that had already been published or whether the author of that book had borrowed such and such an element from Kant's written doctrine or his lectures (as they were disseminated by the students' notes), that we rediscover in the *Anthropology*, its place of origin. It would seem, for example, that Ith was fully acquainted with all of Kant's works (which he often quotes in his *Versuch einer* [7] *Anthropologie*)*; Schmidt also refers to it.**

But all this cross-checking barely manages to scratch the surface; the central issue—the relationship between anthropology and critical thinking—remains untouched. Yet, however inconclusive it may be, this evidence should not be overlooked: by comparing what it teaches us with the texts of the *Anthropology* and those of the *Critique*, we should be able to see how Kant's last work engages with the series of precritical researches, with the whole of the critical enterprise itself and with the group of works that, in the same period, sought to define a specific type of knowledge of man, as well as how, in a paradoxical fashion, those three levels of engagement make the *Anthropology* contemporary with what came before the *Critique*, with what the *Critique* accomplishes, and with what would soon be rid of it.

For this reason, it is impossible to make a clear distinction between the genetic perspective and the structural method in the

---

* Ith refers to Kant I, on p. 12; II, on pages 135, 146, 169, and 341. [Johann Samuel Ith from Bern, (1747–1813), *Versuch einer Anthropologie oder Philosophie des Menschen*, in zwei Theilen, Bern, Emanuel Haller, 1794–1795; See first part, p. 12; second part, pp. 135, 146, 169, and 341.]

** Schmid cites Kant I, p. 22. [See *Empirische Psychologie*, op. cit.]

analysis of this work: we are dealing with a text which, in the thickness of its many layers, its definitive presence and the particular balance of its elements, is contemporary with each phase of the movement that it concludes. Only a genetic study of the whole of the critical enterprise, or, if not that, then a reconstruction of the movement of the whole, could register the finality of the form in which it was achieved and dissolved. Conversely, if the structure of the anthropologico-critical relations could be precisely defined, then only this could uncover the genesis which was to culminate in that final stability—or penultimate, if it is indeed the case that the *Opus Postumum* was already making the first steps on the ground, at last regained, of transcendental philosophy.

Let us first deal with the question of dates. A number[8] of different clues give a fairly accurate indication of when Kant wrote the final draft of the *Anthopology*, which was published by Nicolovius in October, 1798:

1) In a letter to Christoph Wilhelm Hufeland, written in the last fortnight of March 1797, Kant thanks his correspondent for sending the book he had just received: the *Makrobiotik oder die Kunst das menschliche Leben zu verlängern* (Jena, 1796).[9] Kant promises to read the book slowly: "both so that he might conserve his appetite and be sure to grasp the bold and uplifting ideas on the strength of the moral disposition which animates physical man, which he intended to make use of in the *Anthropology*."*

---

* *Kants Werke* (Cassirer X, p. 299). [*Briefe von und an Kant*, in *Immanuel Kants Werke*, edited by Ernst Cassirer, Berlin, B. Cassirer, 1912–1921; vol. IX: 1748–1789; vol. X: 1790–1803. See the letter to Hufeland dated *"nach d. 15. März 1797,"* [740] (704), in *AA*, vol. XII, pp. 148–149.]

2) By September 20ᵗʰ, 1797, work on the *Anthropology* was far enough advanced for Kant's circle of friends and correspondents to begin looking forward to a new book. "Your *Anthropology* will be received with great pleasure," wrote Biester; and, probably on the assumption that the final draft was already complete, he added: "How wonderful that you'll be sending your text to the printers by the end of the year—we've all been looking forward to reading it for such a long time."*

3) On the 5ᵗʰ November of the same year, Tieftrunk wrote to ask if there was any news on the book, expressing some surprise that it hadn't yet appeared: "The public is expecting an *Anthropology* from you; will it be published soon?"**

4) In fact, it is hard to know for sure whether or not the final draft was finished at this point. Kant may have been preoccupied with going over the proofs of the *Conflict of the Faculties*,***10 but his correspondence shows him to be equally eager for any feedback on

---

* *Kants Schriften*, ([illegible word, probably "Ak"], III, p. 217). [See also *AA, Briefwechsel: Dritter Band*, vol. XII, the third volume of Kant's correspondence in the Academy Edition. See in particular letter 778 [739], p. 202. In the Vrin edition, Foucault quotes from the Cassirer edition of *Kants Werke*, vol. X, which does not include all of Kant's letters.]

** Ibid. [See *AA*, op. cit., vol. XII, letter 787 [748], p. 219. Fragments of this letter are published in Immanuel Kant, *Correspondence*, translated and edited by Arnulf Zweig, in *The Cambridge edition of the works of Immanuel Kant*, Cambridge University Press, Cambridge, 1999, pp. 529–534.]

*** See *Kants Werke* (Cassirer, X, p. 346, p. 348). [See "Letter to Friedrich Nicolovius," May 9, 1798, n° 208 [807], in Kant, *Correspondence*, op. cit., pp. 546–547 and "Brief an Carl Friedrich Staüdlin," July 1, 1798, n° 811 [772] in *AA*, vol. XII, op. cit., p. 248.]

the *Anthropology*. When, in a letter written on October 13th, 1797, Kant alludes to the possibility that he might be dying, he suggests that Tieftrunk[11] read the two texts that Professor Gensichen[12] was to look after. One was finished—and had been for two years—the other was almost complete.* It is extremely unlikely that these manuscripts had anything to do with the *Anthropology*—the term *Abhandlung*[13] would not usually be used to refer to a text of such length. In fact, Kant is alluding to two sections of the *Conflict of the Faculties*.[14] Should we therefore presume that the work on the final draft of the *Anthropology* [had not yet begun?][15] Or, on the contrary, that it was already complete and on its way to the publishers?

5) Schöndörffer[16] makes much of the fact that, in the manuscript of the *Anthropology*, Dr. Less[17] is not identified by name: in the section on Albrecht Haller, he is referred to only as a "well-known theologian and ex-colleague (of Haller's) from the university," while in the published text he is named as Dr. Less.** Since Dr. Less died in 1797, we can assume that Kant had not wanted to refer to him by name while he was still living; it follows, then, that the news of his death must have reached him in the stretch of time between the completion of the manuscript and when it was sent to the printer.

6) Both more important and more convincing is the fact that a number of passages from the manuscript found their way, more or less unchanged, into the published text. *Von der Macht des Gemüts durch den blossen Vorsatz seiner krankhaften Gefühle Meister zu sein—*

---

* *Kants Werke*, (Cassirer X, p. 329). [See "Letter to Johann Heinrich Tieftrunk," October 13, 1797, in Emmanuel Kant, *Correspondence*, op. cit., pp. 527–528].

** *Anthropology*, p. 22.

this text makes up the third section of the *Conflict of the Faculties*.[18] In a letter dated April 17th, 1797, Kant talks about the theme of the book as if it had suddenly occurred to him. He had just entered his seventy-forth year and, happily, had so far been spared any kind of illness; it is this which prompts him to speak of *"psychologische Arzneimittel."** It is a fact that his previous letter to Hufeland (written at the end of March)[19] makes no mention of it. It was his reading of the *Makriobiotik* that was decisive, as the "Response to Hufeland" which opens the *Von der Macht des Gemüts* indicates.[20] That text was published in the *Journal der praktischen Arzneikunde und Wundarzneikunst* (4te Stück, V Band. 1798),[21] along with others texts lifted from the *Anthropology*.** We can therefore assume that the final draft had been or was almost complete by the time Kant wrote the article for Hufeland's periodical.

7) A note in the printed text refers to *Von der Macht des Gemüts*.*** Now, this note does not appear in the manuscript held at

---

* *Kants Werke*, Cassirer, X, p. 300. [See "Letter to Christoph Wilhelm Hufeland," April 19, 1797 in *AA*, XII, op. cit. p. 157–158. The letter Foucault is referring to is dated April 19th. *Psychologisches Arzneimittel* (Psychological Drug), p. 158.]

** It essentially has to do with a passage of the manuscript at § 26, where sleep is defined as a relaxation of the muscles and waking as a condition of strain and contraction. The proof of this is that when a man who has only just been woken up is measured standing up, he is found to be "about half an inch" taller than the same man measured after having lain awake in bed for a while. [See *Anthropology*, p. 58.]

*** *Anthropology*, p. 106. [In a note in the draft of his translation Foucault cites: *Von der Macht des Gemüts seiner krankhaften Gefühlen Meister zu sein (1798)*. See Part III of *The Conflict of the Faculties*, (op. cit.), entitled "On the Power of the Mind to Master its Morbid Feelings by sheer Resolution," pp. 313–327.]

Rostock, which leads us to presume that, at the time he wrote it, Kant had not yet finished—and perhaps had not even begun—work on the article meant for Hufeland.

8) As others have remarked, a note in the margin of the manuscript refers to a work by Hearne, two German translations of which were published in 1797. Kant must therefore have read them in the second half of that year, once the manuscript was finished. But, once again, we should bear in mind that Kant had already cited Hearne in *Religion within the Boundaries of Mere Reason.** It is therefore possible that the note was a recollection and an addition.

All of this information indicates a fairly precise date: Kant must have been putting the final touches to the manuscript of the *Anthropology* in the first half of 1797—perhaps in the first three or four months of that year. It seems that the sudden flash of inspiration which gave rise to *Von der Macht* did not interrupt work on a draft which was already in its last stages, though it is likely that it delayed the printing and the final corrections. It was once *Von der Macht* was finished and perhaps even sent off to Hufeland that the last changes to the *Anthropology* were made (passages that appeared twice were cut out, references were

---

* Cf. Kants, *Werke*, Ak., p. 354, fn.1. [See Oswald Külpe's footnote in *Anthropologie, AA*, vol. VII, op. cit., p. 354. See also "Religion within the Boundaries of Mere Reason and Other Writings," translated by George Di Giovanni, in *Religion and Rational Theology*, op. cit., p. 80, and Samuel Hearne, *A Journey from Prince of Wales Fort in Hudson's Bay to the Northern Ocean*, Londres, Cadell, 1795 (*Hearne's Reise von dem Prinz von Wallis-fort an der Hudsons-Bay bis zu dem Eismeere, in den jahren 1769 bis 1772. Aus dem englischen übersetzt. Mit anmerkungen von Johann Reinhold*, Berlin, Vossische buchhandlung, 1797). Samuel Hearne (1745–1792), was an English seaman in the service of the Hudson Bay Company.]

added), and either instructions were given to the printer or the corrections were made directly on the proofs.[22]

In itself, the exact date of the text is neither entirely without interest nor is it altogether conclusive. It acquires its meaning—and shows the extent to which it is meaningful—only if we consider the text, as it was at this point in time, alongside both texts written in the same period as well as those contemporaneous with the first lectures in *Anthropology*. If we accept that the text's origins lie in 1772, sandwiched between *Kant's Inaugural Dissertation of 1770*[23] and the *On the Various Races of Mankind*,[24] then we see that the *Anthropology* emerged over the course of the years which appear to have brought the precritical period to a close and heralded the Copernican revolution.

One thing, in any case, is certain: the text published in 1798 fits in easily with a number of different writings from the precritical period:

a) *Observations on the Feeling of the Beautiful and the Sublime* (1764). The similarities between this text and the *Anthropology* have already been carefully and precisely detailed by R. Kempf.* They are worth noting for the analysis of the temperaments. To be sure, from time to time, the angle adopted in the two texts is completely different: in the *Observations*, the take on the temperaments is structured around the problem of moral feeling, their classification having been taken as given; the description in the *Anthropology*, on the other hand, is determined by a kind of deduction of the temperaments,

---

* *Observations sur le beau et le sublime*, translated by R. Kempf, (Paris 1959). [E. Kant, *Observations sur le sentiment du beau et du sublime*, Paris, Vrin, 1953, 1992, ibid., pp. IX–XV. See *Observations on the Feeling of the Beautiful and Sublime*, translated by John T. Goldthwait, Berkeley and London, University of California Press, 2003.]

which takes as its starting point the patterns of tension and release of activity and of feeling.* Nevertheless, the content is surprisingly similar, even down to the expressions and the choice of words. On the topic of the *choleric temperament*, for example, we read in the *Observations* that: *"sein Wohlwollen ist Höflichkeit, seine Achtung Zeremonie"***; and in the *Anthropology*: *"er ist höflich aber mit Zeremonie."* There are similar coincidences around the discussions of the male and female character,*** as well as of the distinctive traits that characterise the different nationalities.**** All of which clearly indicates the distant origin of the text, the permanence of those elements which the passage of time left quite literally untouched.

b) *An Essay on the Maladies of the Mind* (1764). Here, again, there are many common elements: the distinction***** between

---

* *Anthropology*, pp. 186 and ff.

** *Beobachtungen*, Cassirer, vol. II, p. 260 and ff. [In *Kants Werke*, edited by Ernst Cassirer, vol. II, Berlin, 1912. *"Sein Wohlwollen ist Höflichkeit, seine Achtung Zeremonie, seine Liebe ausgesonnene Schmeichelei,"* *Beobachtungen über das Gefühl des Schönen und Erhabenen*, in *AA*, vol. II, *Vorkritische Schriften 1757–177*, p. 223. "His benevolence is politeness, his respect ceremony, his love excogitated flattery," *Observations on the Feeling of the Beautiful and Sublime*, op. cit., p. 69.] *Anthropologie*, p. 189. ["He is avaricious so as order not to be stingy; polite, with ceremony," ibid.]

*** *Beobachtungen*, ibid., p. 269 and ff. [in *AA*, vol. II, p. 228 and ff. *Observations on the Feeling of the Beautiful and Sublime*, op. cit., p. 76 and ff.] *Anthropologie*, p. 204 and ff. [*The Character of the Sexes*].

**** *Beobachtungen*, ibid., p. 286 and ff. [In *AA*, vol. II, p. 243 and ff. *Observations on the Feeling of the Beautiful and Sublime*, op. cit., p. 97 and ff.] *Anthropology*, p. 213 and ff. [*The Character of the Peoples*].

***** *Versuch*. Cassirer. II., pp. 304–305. [See *Versuch über die Krankheiten des Kopfes*, in *AA*, Bd. II, op. cit., p. 263.] *Anthropology*, p. 96 and ff.

Torheit and *Narrheit*: "*Der Tor ist nicht weise, der Narr ist nicht klug*";[25] the distinction between the illnesses of weakness (*Ohnmacht*), and those of perturbation (*Verkehrtheit*) reappears in the *Anthropology*, its meaning unchanged, as the opposition between mental deficiencies (*Gemütsschwäche*)* and mental illnesses (*Gemütskrankheiten*). It is however worth noting that certain types of madness which, in the *Anthropology*, come under deficiencies (*Dummheit*,[26] *Albernheit*,[27] *Jorheit*[28]) are in the *Essay* put to one side and as it were devalorised with regard to the real illnesses deserving of our sympathy; they are described as "*diese ekelhafte Krankheiten.*"** On the other hand, in the *Anthropology* the important distinction between the major mental illnesses, while formulated in the same terms as those of the earlier *Essay*, is now given a radically different meaning. The *Essay*'s classification is simple: the *Verrückung* alters the concepts of experience, and this gives rise to illusions, as in hypochondria***; delirium (*Wahnsinn*) affects judgement, as in the case of the melancholic****; finally, dementia (*Wahnwitz*) impacts on reason and its capacity to make judgements.***** In the *Anthropology*, this classification has been modified: its organizing concepts are

---

* Ibid., pp. 306–307. [*Versuch über die Krankheiten des Kopfes*, in *AA*, vol. II, p. 263: "*Ich theile diese Krankheiten zwiefach ein, in die der Ohnmacht und in die der Verkehrtheit*" ("I divide these diseases up into two categories: unconsciousness and wrongness"). See *Anthropology*, pp. 98–111: B. *On Mental Deficiencies in the Cognitive Faculty; C. On Mental Illnesses.*]

** Ibid., p. 304. [*Versuch über die Krankheiten des Kopfes*, in *AA*, vol. II, p. 260. "*diese ekelhafte Krankheiten:* repulsive illnesses."]

*** Ibid., p. 309. [In *AA*, vol. II, p. 265.]

**** Ibid., p. 312. [In *AA*, vol. II, p. 268.]

***** Ibid., p. 313. [In *AA*, vol. II, p. 268.]

those relating to possible experience, while the notions of *amentia, dementia, insania,* and *vesania** are bracketed under the general heading of alienation (*Verrückung*), as they are in Sauvage, or Linné. The affinity between the text of the *Anthropology* and that of the *Essay* is still obvious, but here we have a clearer indication of how the text was made to fit with the critical discoveries and the scientific developments of the time.

c) It is also worth noting the echo** of a text from 1771, in which Kant acknowledges a dissertation by Moscati:[29] "Von dem körperlichen Unterschiede zwischen der[30] Struktur der Tiere und Menschen."[31] Twenty-six years on, Kant evokes the difficult and, in his eyes, futile problem of primitive man's upright posture.

d) *Of the Different Human Races* (1775).[32] The *Anthropology* grants less than a page to the problem dealt with in the *Essay*, and simply refers the reader to a text by Girtanner, who had recently provided a summary of Kant's ideas in his dissertation: "Über das kantische Prinzip für die Naturgeschichte."*** But *Of the Different Human Races* concludes with a brief paragraph**** which is important

---

* *Anthropology*, pp. 109–110. [Madness; insanity; delirium; lunacy.]

** *Anthropology*, p. 226.

*** Göttingen, 1796. [Christ. G. Girtanner, a Professor at Göttingen, *Über das kantische Prinzip für die Naturgeschichte*, Göttingen, Vandenhoeck, 1796. See also *Kants Bestimmung des Begriffes einer Menschenrassem* in Ernst Cassirer, *Anthropology*, vol. 8, pp. 91–106.]

**** Cassirer vol. II, pp. 459–460. [*AA*, vol. 2, p. 443: "*Die physische Geographie, die ich hierdurch ankündige, gehört zu einer Idee, welche ich mir von einem nütlichen akademischen Unterricht mache, den ich die Vorübung in der Kenntnis der Welt nennen kann.*" ("The physical geography which I hereby announce, is part of an idea which I have about useful academic teaching, which I might call the preliminary practice to the knowledge of the world.")]

for our understanding of the place given to *Anthropology* in the organization of knowledge. *Of the Different Human Races* was intended to get the first lecture in physical geography of the summer semester 1775 "under way"—and in this sense it belongs to that discipline. But geography is not an end in itself, it does not simply refer to itself: as an exercise, it serves as a preliminary introduction to the knowledge of the world (*Weltkenntniss*) that in the *Anthropology* Kant would later make synonymous with a knowledge of man. This constitution of a *Weltkenntniss* has two specific features:

1) It should furnish "all acquired knowledge and skill"* with a pragmatic element, in such a way that, it serves not only to contribute to our schooling,[33] but also works as a tool to help organize and guide our concrete existence.[34]

2) To do so, the two domains in which knowledge is exercised—Nature and Man—must not be taken to be big themes, about which we might occasionally make a few impassioned remarks; rather, they should be conceived in cosmological terms; that is, in relation to the whole of which they are a part, and within which they take their place and situate themselves (*darin ein jeder selbst seine Stelle einnimmt*).[35]

These themes are close to those mentioned in the *Introduction* and the last pages of the *Anthropology*. But, while the thematic content might remain constant (the prevalence of the pragmatic element, the concern that knowledge should consider the world as a unified whole), the texts are structured differently: physical geography and anthropology are no longer set alongside one another as

---

* The phrase is repeated as such at the beginning of the *Anthropology*, p. 3. ["All cultural progress ... has the goal of applying this acquired knowledge and skill for the world's use." *Anthropology*, p. 3.]

the two symetrical halves of the knowledge of the world articulated on the basis of an opposition between man and nature; the task of directing us toward a *Weltkenntniss* is now the sole responsibility of an anthropology which encounters nature in no other form than that of an already habitable Earth (*Erde*). As a result, the notion of a cosmological perspective that would organize geography and anthropology in advance and by rights,[36] serving as a single reference for both the knowledge of nature and of the knowledge of man, would have to be put to one side to make room for a cosmopolitical perspective with a programmatic value, in which the world is envisaged more as a republic[37] to be built than a cosmos given in advance.

At the other extreme of the Kantian oeuvre, the *Anthropology* is contemporary with a certain number of texts which, when taken together, help to determine when the final draft was completed—or, at least, to establish which were the last additions. Holding on to both ends of the thread in this way, we are perhaps better equipped to tackle an issue that is at once historical and structural, and which is apparent both in the chronology of the texts and in the architectonics of the oeuvre as a whole: the fact, that is, of the contemporaneity of the critical thinking and the anthropological reflection.

What, then, were the issues preoccupying Kant as he prepared the text for publication—this text, so archaic in its concerns, and so remotely rooted in his oeuvre?

1) *The final installment in the correspondence with Jakob Sigismund Beck.*[38] The last letter of philosophical interest that Kant wrote to Beck is dated July 1st, 1794. It deals with what Beck called the

Beilegung—the relating of a representation, as a determination of the subject, to an object distinct from it, by which means it becomes cognition.[39] Kant makes the point that the representation does not "befit" the object but that a relation to something else befits the representation, whereby it becomes communicable to other people.[40] He also stresses that grasping (*apprehensio*) a given multiplicity and its reception in the unity of consciousness (*apperceptio*) amounts to the very same thing as the representation of a composite that is possible only through composition.[41] And it is only from the point of view of this composition that we can communicate with one another: in other words, we are able to communicate with one another because of this composition, it is its relationship to the object that renders the representation valid for everyone and everywhere communicable; which does not mean we are exempt from producing the composition ourselves. The major themes of the *Critique*—the relation to the object, the synthesis of the manifold, the universal validity of representation—are in this way directly related to the problem of communication. The transcendental synthesis is only ever given as balanced in the possibility of an empirical division manifested in the double form of agreement (*Übereinstimmung*) and communication (*Mitteilung*). In what only appears to be a contradiction, the fact that a representation can be assigned to more than one thing, and that such multiplicity is not already given as bound up in itself, is what ensures that one representation can always be exchanged for another: "Wir können aber nur das verstehen und anderen mitteilen, was wir selbst machen können."*

---

* Cassirer, X, pp. 248–249. [In *Correspondence*, op. cit.: "But we can only understand and communicate to others what we ourselves can *produce*," p. 482.]

There the philosophical correspondence with Beck ends. "I notice," writes Kant in conclusion to his letter, "that I do not even entirely understand myself"; he goes onto express his hope that a mathematician such as Beck might be in a position to shed a sufficiently bright light on "this simple, thin thread of our cognitive faculty."[42] The dialogue with Beck would not be renewed in his lifetime, but it did, in fact, continue—in one direction at least. For Beck would write three more letters to Kant. The first is once again concerned with the problem addressed in the last letter: the synthetic unity of consciousness, representation which has no link to the object outside the act of representation itself.* The second considers two themes**: on the one hand, the irreducibility of sensibility and understanding (Is the object that affects the senses a thing in itself or phenomenon?[43] Can understanding be applied to objects without the condition of sensibility? Is the role of sensibility to affect the subject and of understanding to relate that subjective sensation to an object?); on the other, the relationship between theory and practice (In practical awareness, is man, who raises himself above nature, still a *Naturgegenstand*?).[44] Finally, along with the problem of the original activity of understanding, the third letter considers the Fichtian error of never distinguishing between practical and theoretical philosophy.*** To all of this, Kant gave no reply—or at least not directly. A brief missive to Tieftrunk

---

* Letter dated September 16th, 1794. Cassirer, vol. X, pp. 251–252. [In *AA*, vol. XI, Letter 639 (604), pp. 523–525; not translated in *Correspondence*.]

** Letter dated June 20th, 1797. [In *AA*, vol. XII, letter 754 (717), pp. 162–171; in *Correspondence* the letter has been cut, pp. 512–515.]

*** Letter dated June 24th, 1797. Cassirer, vol. X, pp. 310–313. [*Correspondence*, pp. 517–520, see especially pp. 518–519.]

alludes to his difficulties with Beck;[45] the real response, however, is to be found in the *Anthropology*, partly in the published text, and partly in a long passage in the manuscript which was omitted from the final version.

a) It is important to note the range and the consistency given to the realm of sensibility in the published text. To be sure, a faculty of apprehension (*Auffassungsvermögen*) exists which seems to act in productive capacity with regard to sensibility, in that it is capable of generating intuition (*die Anschauung hervorzubringen*).[46] Here, though, we are dealing with understanding considered as a faculty of cognition in general.* But, taken in the narrower sense, understanding is opposed to sensible intuition which remains absolutely irreducible to it to the extent that imagination as the reproductive faculty is organized on the basis of the originary and insurmountable productivity of sensible intuition.** But this does not mean that the faculty of primary productivity—which understanding can neither reduce or construct—is any less fundamentally linked to the subject through the a priori forms of intuition. The opposition between understanding and sensibility does not threaten the unity that Beck, insisting on their identity, would call *"das Erfahrende."*[47] "Ich als denkendes Wesen bin zwar mit mir als Sinnenwesen ein und dasselbe Subject."***

In the *Anthropology*, Kant is also careful to distinguish between inner sense and apperception. The one is defined as

---

* *Anthropology*, p. 26 ff.

** Ibid., p. 60.

*** Ibid., p. 33. ["It is true that I as a thinking being am one and the same subject with myself as a sensing being."]

consciousness of what man does; the other as consciousness of what he feels.* These definitions overlap with those of the *Critique*, but there is nevertheless a difference. Apperception, which in the *Critique* is reduced to the simplicity of an "I think,"** is here related to the originary activity of the subject, while inner sense—which in the *Critique* was analysed on the basis of the a priori of time***—is given here in the primitive diversity of a "*Gedankenspiel*"****[48] that operates beyond the mastery of the subject, and which makes of inner sense more the sign of an initial passivity than a constituting activity.

b) In the unpublished text, Kant expands in more detail on the problem of self-cognition.[49] Inner sense, thus defined as empirical consciousness, cannot perceive the 'I' other than as an object—the 'I' observed which is now taken to be the *Inbegriff*[50] of the objects of inner perception. Apperception, on the other hand, is defined—in a sense much closer to that of the *Critique*—by intellectual self-consciousness;[51] it thus refers neither to any given object, nor to any intuitive content. It has to do with nothing other than an act undertaken by the determining subject, and to this extent belongs not to Psychology, nor to Anthropology, but to Logic. Whence the great danger, evoked by Fichte, of the subject dividing into two forms of subjectivity that would no longer able to communicate with one another other than on the unequal footing of

---

* Ibid.

** *The Paralogisms of Pure Reason* [in French in the text], Cassirer, vol. III, p. 272 and ff. [See I. Kant, *Critique of Pure Reason*, translated and edited by Paul Guyer and Allen W. Wood, Cambridge University Press, Cambridge, 1998, p. 409 and ff.]

*** Refutation of Idealism [in French in the text], ibid. p. 200. [*Critique of Pure Reason*, op. cit., p. 326.]

**** *Anthropology*, p. 32.

subject to object.* This, Kant acknowledged, is a "great difficulty." Still, we should bear in mind that what is in question is not a "*doppeltes Ich*," but a "*doppeltes Bewusstsein dieses Ich*."** Thus the 'I' preserves its unity, and if, at times, it presents itself to consciousness as something perceived and, at others, in the form of a judgement, this is because it is self-affecting; being, in one and the same gesture, both "*das bestimmende Subjekt*" and "*das sich selbst bestimmende Subjekt*." In this way, a sensibility irreducible to understanding manages to avert the danger of the division of the subject. There is no need to bracket the whole of the field of experience under the general heading of understanding, nor to make understanding the *Erfahrende* par excellence, nor, finally, to put the orginary form of "*Verstandes-Verfahren*" into categories—all extreme solutions which Beck, impressed by his reading of Fichte, thought it necessary to implement if the division of the Kantian subject was to be avoided.

Beck's letters, which Kant received just as he was completing the draft of the definitive text of the *Anthropology* (or very shortly before), are at the origin of those responses that can be discerned both in the manuscript and the published work. It is possible that those passages were omitted from the published text because they looked too much like reponses to Beck, and to the problems he raised, to be included in an *Anthropology* in the proper sense. At the same time, however peripheral it may have been, the debate with

---

* Fichte, *Zweite Einleitung in die Wissenschaftslehre* (Sämtliche Werke, I., p. 457 and ff.) [J.G. Fichtes Werke, *herausgegeben von Emmanuel Hermann Fichte*, vol. I, de Gruyter, Berlin, 1971. See J.G. Fichte, *Science of Knowledge with the First and Second Introductions*, edited and translated by Peter Heath and John Lachs, Cambridge University Press, Cambridge, 1982, p. 33 and ff.]

** *Anthropology*, p. 30 and ff. [fn 24: "a double I" and "a doubled consciousness of this I," p. 31.]

Beck enabled Kant to define the space in which an anthropology, in general, could occupy: a space in which self-observation bears not upon the subject as such, nor upon the pure 'I' of the synthesis, but upon "a 'I'" that is object and present *solely* in its *singular* phenomenal truth. But this "'I'-object," given to sense in the form of time, is no stranger to the determining subject; for it is ultimately nothing more than the subject as it is affected by itself. Far from the space of anthropology being that of the mechanism of nature and extrinsic determinations (in which case it would be a "physiology"), it is entirely taken over by the presence of a deaf, unbound, and often errant freedom which operates in the domain of originary passivity. In short, we see a field proper to anthropology being sketched out, where the concrete unity of the syntheses and of passivity, of the affected and the constituting, are given as phenomena in the form of time.

But locating the place of anthropology in this way is possible only from the point of view of transcendental reflection. We can therefore see why Kant gave up the idea of publishing a text so foreign, if not to the problem of anthropology, then certainly to its own particular level of reflection. The *Anthropology* should only contain that which pertains to its own level: the analysis of the concrete forms of self-observation. But, if we look at them together, the unpublished and the published texts constitute two different layers of a unified thought process which, in a single move, responds to Beck, wards off the Fichtian danger, and outlines, or as it were hollows out, the possible place for an anthropology.

2) *The discussions on the subject of the metaphysics of Law.* Since the sixteenth century, juridical thought has been concerned either with defining the individual's relationship to the State in its general form or the relationship between the individual and the thing

in the abstract form of property. But here we have, in the second half of the eighteenth century, an investigation into the forms of ownership amongst individuals in the concrete and particular forms of the couple, the family group, the home, and the household: how can civil society, which is presupposed by the bourgeoisie both as its foundation and its justification, be divided into discrete units which no longer have anything to do with the feudal model but which are solid enough to withstand its final dissolution? Christian Gottfried Schütz[52] was concerned to find, reading Kant's *Metaphysics of Morals*,[53] ownership amongst individuals so closely modeled on the main forms of rights over things. Indeed, Kant makes room for these forms of ownership in a section entitled "Von dem auf dingliche Art persönlichen Recht,"[54] which is divided into three parts according to the three types of aquisition: a man acquires (*erwirbt*) a wife; a couple acquires children; a family acquires domestics.* Now, Schütz refused to accept that in matrimony "the woman becomes a thing which belongs to the man";[55] the kind of satisfaction which a man can gain from his wife in the context of a marriage prevents her from being reduced to such a primitively simple status; the objectification of the other only has any truth in cannibalism: marriage and the rights that it accords do not make people into "*res fungibiles.*" The same goes for servants, who could only be considered things if their capture, and the right to capture them, were written into the fundamental rules of civil society. In short, the problem which Schütz identifies in its various forms comes down to the constitution of these concrete little islands in bourgeois society which are recognised neither by the rights of the people nor by the

---

* *Die Metaphysik der Sitten*, Cassirer, vol. VII, p. 80 and ff. [*The Metaphysics of Morals*, op. cit., § 23, p. 426.]

right to the ownership of things: spontaenous syntheses that neither a theory of contract, nor an analysis of appropriation can quite account for; fringes of the law where domination is neither of the order of sovereignty nor of ownership.

In a letter to Schütz dated July 10th, 1797—written at the time when he was probably finishing the final draft of the *Anthropology*—Kant responds to the two objections put to him: the *mutuum adjutorium* of sexual relations is the necessary legal consequence of marriage, which is to say that objectification in the relationship between a man and a woman is not a fact which founds the law but a fact which arises from a state of law, a state of law which is contested only if that fact occurs outside of the law; falling beyond or falling short of the bounds of marriage, the libertinage of a *Freidenker* amounts to the same thing, all that changes is its anthropological form. But, conversely, if the moral significance of sexual relations changes dramatically according to whether or not they take place within the juridical structure of a marriage, the content of the act itself remains the same; one partner becomes a thing for the other, an a*djutorium* of his pleasure. The law authorises the fact: but, in so doing, it does not alter the content, which remains unchanged.

The same goes for the relationship with servants: evidently we are dealing here with people, but from a juridical point of view the relationship is one of ownership. That someone has another person in his possession represents a *jus in re*:[56] the servant—in contrast to a man who works in the day and goes home at night—is an integral part of the *Hauswesen*.[57] The law might treat the person as a thing; it does not follow, however, that the person has become a thing; rather, it establishes a relationship between two people that is of the same order as that between a person and a thing. In his objections, Schütz confuses the moral perspective with the legal perspective, the human being with the subject of the law—a distinction which Kant rigorously reinstates in his response.*

Nevertheless, Schütz's objection goes to the very heart of the anthropological concern, which is itself a point of convergence and divergence between law and moral principle. The *Anthropology* is *pragmatic* in the sense that it does not conceive of man as belonging to the moral republic[58] of souls (which would make it *practical*), nor to a civil society made up of legal subjects (which would make it *juridical*); instead, man is considered to be a "citizen of the world,"[59] as belonging, that is, to the realm of the concrete universal, in which the legal subject is determined by and submits to certain laws, but is at the same time a human being who, in his or her freedom, acts according a universal moral code. To be a "citizen of the world" is to belong to a realm that is as concrete as an ensemble of precise juridical rules, themselves as universal as moral law. Thus, to say that anthropology is pragmatic, and to say that it envisages man as a citizen of the world, effectively amounts to saying the same thing. In such conditions, it falls to anthropology to show how a juridical relationship of the order of a possession, which is to say a *jus rerum*, manages to preserve the moral kernel of a person construed as a free subject. To preserve it, though not without compromising it at the same time.

Such is the paradox of the relations between men and women as they are described in the *Anthropology***: in her natural state, a woman is nothing more than a *Haustier*,[60] a domestic animal; yet, already in primitive polygamy, a game is initiated whereby, even if

* Letter dated June, 10th 1797. Cassirer X. p. 314–316. [In *AA*, vol. XII, 761 (724), pp. 181–183.]

** *Anthropology*, p. 204 and ff.

women are objectified, the possibility of them arguing amongst themselves, of rivalry or coquetery, makes the owner into the object of their struggles; the ruses of the harem soon managed to substitute the arbitrary rule of the master for his arbitrary submission to whoever happens to be the mistress this time around. The monogamous structure of civilised society does not liberate woman from her status as a possession, far from it: her infidelity, which nullifies the relationship of ownership, actually authorises the man to destroy the object of the relation now rendered void: that is, he is authorised to kill the woman. But jealousy, as a violent form of interaction which objectifies a woman to the point where she can simply be destroyed, is also a recognition of her value; indeed, only the absence of jealousy could reduce a woman to a piece of merchandise, where she would be interchangeable with any another. The right to be jealous—to the point of murder—is an acknowledgement of a woman's moral freedom. Now, the first claim of this freedom is to escape the consequences of such jealousy; if a woman is to prove that she is something more than a thing, she has to incite a form of jealousy that is powerless in the face of the irrepressible exercise of her freedom; hence the introduction of *gallantry* within the law of monogamy, which serves to strike a balance between the *jus rerum* whereby a wife is owned by her husband, and the moral law whereby everyone is a free subject. To strike a balance is however not the same as reaching an end, nor does it follow that things are balanced equally. For gallantry is nothing more than a muddle of pretensions: the man's, to restrict the woman's freedom by marrying her; the woman's, to exercise her power over the man in spite of marriage. Thus a whole network of relations are woven together, where neither the law nor morality are ever present in their pure states, but where their intersection creates the space in which human action is played out; this is its concrete latitude. This is not the level of fundamental freedom, nor that of legal rule. What emerges is a sort of pragmatic freedom which is all about pretensions and ruses, dishonourable intentions and dissimulation, secret attempts to gain control, and compromises reached.

No doubt Kant had all of this in mind when, in the Preface to the *Anthropology*, he states as his object what man makes of himself—or can and should make of himself—as a free-acting being ("*freihandelndes Wesen*"):[61] the commerce of freedom with itself, finding itself restricted by the movement by which it is affirmed; *manipulation*, where the negotiations of exchange are never interrupted by the straightforward recognition of value. Treating man as a "*freihandelndes Wesen*," the *Anthropology* uncovers a whole zone of "free-exchange," where man trades his second-hand freedoms, connecting with others by way of an unspoken and uninterrupted commerce which ensures that he is at home anywhere on earth. A citizen of the world.

3) *The correspondence with Hufeland and the third section of the Conflict of the Faculties.* The letters Kant wrote while working on the final draft of the *Anthropology* show that, in truth, he was less preoccupied by the problems of critical thought—problems which, as he grew older, he was aware of no longer being able to fully grasp—than by a certain form of interrogation in which old age is surprised by and becomes a question in itself: What to make of old age, where one is no longer capable of grasping the subtleties of transcendental thought, and yet still seems to be capable of warding off all kinds of illness? Is this a prolongation of life or its end? Does this age of reason imply a mastery over the precariousness of life? Time is running out, the end is approaching, regardless of anything we might do—could this irrepressible movement somehow be controlled or

bypassed by an active synthesis of reason, which would bring it under the impassive rule of wisdom? This is the third time that the problem of passivity and time is seen to be overshadowing the preparation of the definitive version of the *Anthropology*.

This problem intersects with a text published by Hufeland, entitled "*Makrobiotik* oder die Kunst das menschliche leben zu verlängern."* The text belongs to a whole movement in German medicine illustrated by the work of Reil[62] and Heinroth:[63] a huge anthropological drive to adapt the observation of illnesses to a metaphysics of evil, and to discover by which shared gravitational pull the collapse into pathological mechanism overlaps with freedom's fall into sin.** Hufeland's text, although not quite as radical, is nevertheless in the vicinity of these ideas. For the text, though showing a degree of restraint, is like the pragmatic mirror image of the same ideas: for Hufeland it is a question of "offering moral treatment of physical symptoms" and of demonstrating that "a culture of morality is indispensable to the physical health of human beings."*** Here, in a single stroke, that moralising medicine which, in the tradition of Rousseau, had been a dominant force at the close of the eighteenth century, is realized and its meaning overturned. In this new ethical physiology, the link between health and virtue is not one of natural immediacy, as it was for Tissot, but is given through the universal mastery of reason. Health is the visible plane of an existence where the organic totality is dominated, without remainder and without opposition, by a form of rationality

---

* Iena, 1796. [Jena, op. cit.]

** See Heinroth, Reil and soon [Illegible words] Hoffbauer.

*** Letter from Hufeland to Kant, Cassirer, vol. X, pp. 294–295. [Letter 728 (693), dated December 12th, 1796, in *AA*, pp. 136–137.]

that, beyond any division, is at once ethical and organic; it is the playground of freedom—the space in which freedom can play, but precisely a space that is only constituted by its game. And if in the "pathos" of illness there is something which links it to the passions, it is no longer due to its being too far removed from the calm world of nature, but because of a dip in the spiritual arc of freedom: determinism—freedom unbound—is not quite a cause, but nor is it simply an effect of illness: it is the very process by which illness produces itself, that is to say the process by which organic rationality dismantles itself and, in the sin, renounces its freedom. It is therefore in the good use of freedom that the possibility of "*das menschliche leben zu verlängern*"[64] takes hold, keeping the mechanics of the body from the sinful fall into mechanism.

This new orientation in medicine—soon to become the philosophy of nature—acknowledges its kinship with Kantianism. Hufeland concedes this unreservedly in a letter dated December 12th, 1796, where he tells Kant that has posted him a copy of his *Makrobiotik*. Sending Kant a copy was doubly justified—first, by the fact that Kant was living proof of how it is possible to conserve one's vitality in old age, even in whilst undertaking the most stingent spiritual labours; second, because his oeuvre authorises a knowledge of man which is, at bottom, the veritable anthropology.*

When Hufeland's letter and book arrived—they had been quite considerably delayed, finally reaching him in the middle of March 1797**—Kant was interested in the very same problem. He set about reading Hufeland's book carefully—and slowly, as he wanted to be sure to have fully understood the author's ideas if he was to

---

* Letter from Hufeland to Kant, Cassirer, vol. X, p. 294. [In *AA*, vol. XII, pp. 136–137.]

** Letter from Kant to Hufeland. Cassirer vol. X, p. 299. [In *AA*, vol. XII, pp. 148–149.]

make use of them in his *Anthropology*.* About three weeks later, Kant wrote a letter to Hufeland, telling him everything about his most recent project ("*Mir ist der Gedanke in den Kopf gekommen*")[65] to write a *Regimen* "on the topic of the power exercised by the mind over morbid bodily sensations." He meant to send the work to Hufeland, despite the fact that the book would not be a medical one, but more a reflection on his own personal experience. Kant would make two uses of the *Regimen*: he sent it to Hufeland, who was also given permission to publish it in his *Revue*, either in full or in part, with an introduction and commentary**; it was also to become the third part of the *Conflict of the Faculties****—thereby creating a systematic whole which would study the relationship between the Faculty of Philosophy and the three others. Thus a philosopher's personal contribution to the medical enterprise, to come up with a Regimen, comes to signify, simultaneously and without having undergone any modification, the debate and the division between medical science and philosophical reflection over how to define the everyday art of healthy living.

In actual fact, what dominates the text is not of the order of a debate. While the resolution of the "conflict" between the faculties of philosophy and theology called for nothing less than a "*Friedens-abschluss*,"[66] the relations between philosophy and medicine were, at the outset, placid. Medical prescription and philosophical precept fit together spontaneously in the logic of their nature: a moral

---

* Ibid.

** Letter to Hufeland dated February 6th, 1798. Cassirer, vol. X. p. 340. [*Correspondence*, op. cit., p. 543.]

*** See Letter to Nicolovius dated May 9th, 1798. Cassirer, vol. X, p. 345. [*Correspondence*, op. cit., pp. 546–547.]

and practical philosophy is a "*Universal medizin*" in the sense that, while it cannot meet all needs or serve all purposes, no prescription is written without one. The fact is, with regard to medicine, a moral and practical philosophy is the universal negative (it excludes illness)—which means, with regard to the Regimen, it serves as the universal positive (it defines the laws of preservation in the play of health). Philosophy is the element of universality against which the particulars of medical prescription are always measured: it forms its unprescribable horizon, taking in both health and illness. To be sure, this precedence is masked by the immediacy of human wishes: when we wish for a long and healthy life, only the first of those wishes is unconditional: a sick man pleading for delivrance in death always calls for a reprieve when the moment finally comes; but what is unconditional in the register of the wish takes second place in life: no one dies a natural death when in good health—we might not feel ill, but still, illness is there. Illness is the indispensable "seed of death."* The art of prolonging life is therefore not about scoring a victory over the absolute of death in the comprehensive mastery of life; it is, at the very heart of life, the measured and relative art of managing the relationship between health and illness.

The meaning of this art is perhaps not best expressed in the idea of "the mind's control over pathological sensations." For, sensations being what they are, only their intensity, and the amount of time we spend thinking about them, can be controlled: hypochondria is a form of delirium not in the sense that the "*Krankheitsstoff*" had failed it, but in the sense that the imagination projects the play of its illusions upon it and its simple reality. As for the illnesses themselves,

---

* *Der Streit der Fakultäten.* Cassirer, VII. pp. 412–414. [*The Conflict of the Faculties*, op. cit., pp. 314–315.]

they are susceptible to the mind's control only if they take the form of spasms.* As for the whole of eighteenth century medicine, spasm here does not refer to the involuntary contraction of a hollow organ but, more generally, to all forms of inhibition and acceleration (the former being only the paradoxical effect of the latter) in the natural and regular movements of the organism. Over these movements, or rather over any changes in these movements, the mind has the power to reintroduce equilibrium: the master of his own thought process is also the master of this vital movement which is its organic and indispensable complement. If the mind were immobile, then life would go to sleep—which is to say that it would die (only it is only because we dream that we are kept from dying in our sleep); and if the movement of life risks being thrown off balance, or getting jammed up in a spasm, then the mind must be able to restore it to its proper mobility.

Between the text Kant sent to Hufeland and the *Anthropology* there is direct communication: they are on the same level. Apart from the last two paragraphs, every other paragraph of *Von der Macht*** engages with a theme that is also dealt with in the *Anthropology*: hypochondria, dreams, eating and digestive problems, reflections on what time of day is most conducive to thinking. A long passage on sleep was even deleted from the manuscript of the *Anthropology* because it repeated material from the *Conflict of the Faculties*. Written at the same time, the two texts issue from the same vein of thought.

---

* Ibid., p. 427. [*The Conflict of the Faculties*, op. cit., p. 324.]

** The first is devoted to the "*Vorsatz im Atemziehen*," the second to "*Angewohnheit des Atemziehens mit geschlossenen Lippen*." [See *The Conflict of the Faculties*, op. cit., § 5: *On Overcoming and Preventing Pathological Seizures by a Resolution Concerning Breathing* and § 6: *On the Results of this Habit of Breathing with Closed Lips*, pp. 323–324.]

The research undertaken for Hufeland must have helped Kant to resolve one of the problems that had been hanging over the *Anthropology*: how to articulate an analysis of what the *homo natura* is on the basis of man defined as a free subject. In the *Collegentwürfe* from 1770–1780, the problem is conceived either in terms of a separation: "1. *Kenntniss des Menschen als Naturdinges; 2. als sittlichen Wesen,*"[67] or as a circular argument: "*Weltkentniss ist 1. Naturkenntniss; 2. Menschenkenntniss; aber der Mensch hat auch eine Natur.*"*[68] In the later fragments, we see the solution being sketched out in terms of a "usage" (*Gebrauch*), but the content and the possibility of such a solution remains unclear: "Die Menschenkenntniss hat die Idee zum Grunde dass wir die Natur zu unseren Absichten am besten brauchen können."** It was not until the *Conflict of Faculties* and the draft produced in 1797 that the precise meaning of this *Gebrauch* would emerge. Here, we see how the body's movements, however *conditioning* they may be (of life and death, awakening and sleeping, thinking and not thinking), can nevertheless be *mastered* by the movements of the mind when exercised freely. The theory of "spasms" showed how the passive and spontaneous syntheses of the body could be repeated and rectified in the voluntary movements of the mind. These, however, will never achieve their ends, withdrawing into a sovereignty

---

* *Kants Werke*, Ak. XV, 2te Hälfte, p. 660. [*Collegentwürfe aus den 70er Jahren*, in *AA*, vol. XV: "Knowledge of the World is: 1. Knowledge of nature; 2. Knowledge of Man; but man has a Nature, too."]

** Ibid., p. 801. [*Collegentwürfe aus den 80er Jahren*, in *AA*, vol. XV: "*Die Menschenkenntniss als Weltkenntniss hat die Idee zum Grunde dass wir die Natur zu unseren Absichten am besten brauchen können...*": "The knowledge of man as knowledge of the world is grounded in the idea that we can use nature for our will at the best..."]

that would rule over death. And old age is the sign of this, the necessary decline of that mastery into the spontaneity of the passive syntheses. Old age is not an illness; rather, it is the state in which illness can no longer be mastered—where time, once again, is in control.

We should pause for a moment. And, out of a methodological concern, pretend to read the *Anthropology* as if the *Critique* did not exist—which is what the text itself invites us to do; at no point does the 1798 draft presuppose the existence of the *Critique*. Could it be that the text engages only with the actuality of the system of the postcritical period, and is simply weighed down by memories of the precritical period? A certain number of themes, in any case, were already in place.

1) It was not the aim of the anthropological thinking to bring an end to the definition of a human *Wesen* in naturalist terms: the *Collegentwürfe* from 1770–80 were already saying that "Wir untersuchen hier den Menschen nicht nach dem was er naturlicher Weise ist."* But the *Anthropology* of 1798 transforms this decision into an ongoing method, a resolute readiness to follow a path which, it is clear from the outset, would never lead to the truth of nature. The initial objective of *Anthropology* is to be an *Erforschung*: an exploration of an ensemble never graspable in its totality, never at rest, because always taken up in a movement where nature and freedom are bound up in the *Gebrauch*—one of the meanings of which is given in the word "usage."

---

* Kants Werke, Ak., T. XV, 2, p. 659–660. [In *AA*, vol. 15, part 2: "Our search for Man here is not for what he is in a natural way."]

2) The object of study, then, is not memory as such, but the use made of it.* Not the description of what man is but what he can make of himself. This theme had no doubt been, from the beginning, the very seed of anthropological reflection, as well as the mark of its singularity: "wir untersuchen hier den Menschen... um zu wissen was er aus sich machen und wie man ihn brauchen kann." Such is the programme as it is defined in the *Collegentwürfe*.** In 1798, it has been doubly modified. *Anthropology* is no longer interested in finding out how "man can be used," but "what can be expected of him."*** Moreover, it will investigate what man "can and should" make (*kann und soll*) of himself. Which is to say that the notion of *usage* is wrenched from the level of technical actuality and placed within a double system: of obligation asserted with regard to oneself, and of distance respected with regard to others. Usage is inscribed within the text of a freedom postulated as both singular and universal.

3) The "pragmatic" character of *Anthropology* is thereby defined: according to the *Collegentwürfe*, "Pragmatisch ist die Erkenntnis von der sich ein allgemeiner Gebrauch in der Gesellschaft machen lässt." The pragmatic character was therefore nothing more than the useful universalized. In the 1798 text, however, it is now a certain kind of connection between the *Können* and the *Sollen*. A connection that Practical Reason guaranteed a priori in the Imperative, and

---

* See *Anthropology*, Preface, pp. 3–4.

** *Kants Schriften*. Ak. XV, 2—pp. 659–660. [In *AA*: "Our investigation of Man...aims at knowing what he can make of himself and how he can be employed."]

*** *Anthropology*, p. ? [No number page is indicated; but see *Anthropology* p. 3.]

**** *Kants Schriften*, Ak, XV. 2. p. 660. ["Knowledge is pragmatic if a general social use can be made out of it."]

which in anthropological thinking is ensured by the concrete movement of daily exercise: by the *Spielen*. This notion of *Spielen* is singularly important: man is nature's play*; it is the game that he plays, and is played by it; if he is sometimes played with—as when his senses are deceived—it is because he is playing the victim** of the game, despite it being within his power to be in control, to take back control by feigning his intention. In this way, the game becomes a "*künstlicher Spiel*" and the show he puts on receives its moral justification.*** *Anthropology* thus develops on the basis of this dimension of human exercise that goes from the ambiguity of the *Spiel* (game-toy) to the indecision of the *Kunst* (art-artifice).

4) The book of daily exercise. Not a theoretical book or a school textbook. In a text from the years 1780–90, this opposition is formulated clearly: "Alle Menschen bekommen eine zwiefache Bildung: 1. durch die Schule; 2. durch die Welt."**** This opposition takes form in anthropological teaching—which, after all, amounts to a kind of schooling—thus giving rise to a fundamental tension: the progress of culture, in which the history of the world is summarised, constitutes a school which leads from itself to the knowledge and the practice of the world.***** The world being its own school, the aim of anthropology is to situate man within this instructive context. It will therefore be both, indissociably: the analysis of how man acquires the world (his use, rather than his

* *Anthropology*, pp. 4–5.

** Ibid. [A note is crossed out]

*** Ibid. [A note is crossed out, probably p. 5 and ff.]

**** *Kants Schriften*, Ak., XV. 2, p. 799. [In *AA*. "All human beings receive a twofold education: 1. through school. 2. through the world."]

***** *Anthropology*, p. 4.

knowledge of it), which is to say how he manages to take his place in the world and participate in the game: *Mitspielen*;[69] and, at the same time, the synthesis of the prescriptions and rules that the world imposes on man, which train him, readying him to take control of the game: das *Spiel verstehen*.* *Anthropology* is therefore neither a history of culture nor an analysis of its successive forms, but the practice, at once immediate and imperative, of a culture already given in advance. It teaches man to recognise, within his own culture, what the world teaches him. It has a kinship with *Wilhelm Meister*[70] to the extent that here, too, we find that the World is a School. Yet what in Goethe's novel, and in all of the *Bildungsromane*, is repeated over the length of a whole story, in the *Anthropology* is repeatedly given in the imperious, present, and forever renewed form of daily application. Time rules here, but in the synthesis of the present.

Here then are a few landmarks, on the same latitude as the *Anthropology*, which indicate its particular gradient. Initially, as the *Collegentwürfen* attest, it developed in what was the accepted division between nature and man, freedom and use, school and the world. Now, however, its equiliburum is to be found in the recognition of their unity—a unity which is never again called into question, at least not on the anthropological level. It explores a region where freedom and use are already bound together in the reciprocity of a *usage*, where what one can do and what one must do belong together in the unity of a *play* which measures the one against the other, where the world becomes a school on the basis of the prescriptions of a *culture*. We are touching on the essential point: in *Anthropology*, man is neither a *homo natura*, nor a purely

* *Antropology*. Vorrede [Preface], p. 4.

free subject; he is caught by the syntheses already operated by his relationship to the world.

But could the 1798 text have said *that which* was not yet said in the *Collegentwürfe* if the discourse of the *Anthropology* had remained foreign to the labor and the language of the *Critique*?

Something of the knowledge of the world is thus bound up in this knowledge of man which is anthropology. "*Weltkenntniss ist Menschenkenntniss,*" as a fragment from the 70–80 period affirms.* The preface to the 1798 text assigns itself the object of man as a citizen of the world, *le Weltbürger*.**

And yet, with the exception of the very last pages, the *Anthropology* rarely seems to privilege the theme of man living in the world, of man establishing, through the cosmos, his rights, duties and reciprocities, the limits and exchanges of his citizenship. This lacuna is far more apparent in the published text than in the *Nachlass* fragments. The majority of the analyses, and virtually all of those which appear in the first part of the book, are undertaken not in the cosmopolitical dimension of the *Welt*, but that other—interior—dimension of the *Gemüt*.[71] By the way, in this respect the angle of *Anthropology* is the same as that already adopted by Kant when, on the basis of an encyclopaedic organization, he revealed the link between the three *Critiques*: "Die Vermögen des Gemüts lassen sich nämlich insgesamt auf folgenden drei zurückführen: Erkenntnissvermögen, Gefühl der Lust

---

* *Kants Schriften*, Ak. XV. p. 659. [In *AA*. "Knowledge of the world is the knowledge of man."]

** *Anthropology*, p. 4. ["citizen of the world."]

und Unlust, Begehrungsvermögen."* If it is indeed the case that the *Gemüt* that is in question in the *Anthropology* is the principal element of Kant's exploration, then we are justified in asking a number of questions:

1) How does the study of the *Gemüt* involve knowledge of man as a citizen of the world?

2) If the fundamental and irreducible faculties of the *Gemüt* dictate the organization of the three *Critiques*, and anthropology is, for its part, an analysis of the *Gemüt*, then what is the relationship between anthropological knowledge and critical thought?

3) What distinguishes the investigation of the *Gemüt*, and its faculties, from psychology, whether rational or empirical?

The texts of the *Anthropology* and of the *Critique of Pure Reason* appear to reply to the last question directly—although they do not give the whole of the answer.

We are familiar with the distinction established in the *Architectonic* between rational and empirical psychology.[72] The first belongs to pure philosophy, hence to metaphysics, and so is distinguished from rational physics, as the object of inner sense is distinguished from the object of outer sense. As for empirical psychology, there is a long tradition of placing it within metaphysics;

---

* *Kritik der Urteilskraft.* Cassirer V. p. 225. [*Erste Einleitung in die Kritik der Urteilskraft*, in *Immanuel Kants Werke* in Gemeinschaft mit Hermann Cohen, Artur Buchenau, Otto Buek, Albert Görland, B. Kellermann—herausgegeben von Ernst Cassirer, verlegt bei Bruno Cassirer, Berlin, Bd. V, 1914. See *First Introduction*, in Immanuel Kant, *Critique of the Power of Judgment*, edited by Paul Guyer, translated by Paul Guyer and Eric Matthews, Cambridge University Press, 2000, p. 44: "The faculties of the mind, namely, can all be reduced to the following three: faculty of cognition; feeling of pleasure and displeasure; faculty of desire."]

more importantly, the recent failures of metaphysics have given rise to the belief that the solution to its irresolvable problems were hidden in psychological phemonena pertaining to an empirical study of the soul; in this way, psychology seized upon a lackluster metaphysics in which it had already claimed an unwarranted place. In no circumstances can empirical knowledge provide the principles or shed light on the fundaments of a knowledge issued from pure reason which is, as a consequence, entirely a priori. Empirical psychology must therefore be separated from metaphysics, to which it is foreign. If however such a separation can not be performed straight away, it is because anthropology had to ready psychology for its integration into an empirical science of man, which would then serve as the counterpoint to an empirical science of nature. In this abstract organization, everything seems clear.

And yet, the *Anthropology*, at least in the version available to us, leaves no room for any kind of psychology whatsoever. It explicitly refuses psychology by focusing on the *Gemüt*, and not the exploration of the *Seele*. But what is it that differentiates the two?

a) From a formal point of view, psychology postulates an equivalence between inner sense and apperception, and thus fails to recognise their fundamental difference: apperception is one of the forms of pure consciousness, and is therefore without content, defined only by the *I think*; inner sense, on the other hand, refers to a mode of empirical knowledge, that which enables us to appear to ourselves in an ensemble of phenomena linked by the subjective condition of time.*

b) From the point of view of content, psychology cannot avoid getting caught up in the questions of difference and identity:

---

* *Anthropology*, p. 23 and note.

Does the soul remain the same across time? Is the soul, which makes of itself a condition of experience, affected by experience, by the necessarily temporal sequencing of phenomena?* In other words, is the entire reality of the soul given in the dispersion of phenomena or, on the contrary, in the nonempirical solidity of a substance? So many questions which together show, in a variety of different lights, the confusion between the soul (a metaphysical notion of a simple and immaterial substance), the 'I think' that is pure form, and the ensemble of phenomena that appear to inner sense.

These texts of the *Anthropology* can be placed in a direct line of descent from the *Transcendental Dialectic*.[73] What they denounce is precisely that "inevitable illusion" which the paralogisms acknowledge as such: in our definition of the particular object that is the soul,** we make use of the simple representation of the 'I,' one that is devoid of any content. However, we should note that the paralogisms concern only rational, and not empirical, psychology, which leaves the possibility of a "species of the physiology of inner sense" open—the content of which would depend upon the conditions of all possible experience.*** On the other hand, rational psychology can and must subsist as a discipline, allowing us to escape both materialism and spiritualism, beckoning us away

---

* *Anthropology*, p. 29 and ff.

** *Kritik der reinen Vernunft*. Cassirer III. p. 276. [*The Critique of Pure Reason*, op. cit., p. 414].

*** Ibid., p. 277. [*The Critique of pure reason*, op. cit., p. 415. In the Cassirer edition it reads: "*welche eine Art der Psychologie des inneren Sinnes*," while in Academy Edition we have: "*welche eine Art der Physiologie des inneren Sinnes*." Foucault is refering to the word *Physiologie*].

from this speculation and "*zum fruchtbaren praktischen Gebrauch.*"*
As a result, and even though it appears to target all possible forms
of psychology, the *Anthropology* dismisses only that which had
already been denounced in the *Critique of Pure Reason*. Without
stating it explicitly, it is with regard to rational psychology that the
Anthropology keeps its distance.

What then is the relationship between anthropology and the
two further possibilities which this leaves open—an empirical
psychology and a discipline orientated toward practical application? Does the Anthropology maintain the virtuality of these still
virtual disciplines, keeping them close by but devoid of content,
or are they taken up in its own movement—or, alternatively, are
they too rejected, and made impossible by the realization[74] of the
anthropological program? Two things, at least, are certain: there
is nothing in the text of the *Anthropology* to indicate that an
empirical psychology or a rational psychology in the form of a
"discipline" could be found elsewhere, whether outside or in the
environs of the *Anthropology* itself: there is no indication of a vic-
inal exteriority. But, on the other hand, there is not one element,
section, or chapter of the *Anthropology* which can be identified
with the discipline that the *Dialectic* had forseen or with the
empirical psychology glimpsed from the summit of the *Methodology*.[75] Must we therefore conclude that the Anthropology
constitutes, by a shift in perspectives, both that transcendental
discipline and that empirical knowledge? Or, on the contrary,
that it has made both impracticable, ensuring that neither will
ever get started?

---

* Ibid., p. 286. [*The Critique of pure reason*, op. cit., p. 452: "toward fruitful practical uses."]

It is the *Gemüt*[76] itself that we must now interrogate. Is it, or is it not, of the order of psychology?

It is not *Seele*.[77] On the other hand, it both is and is not *Geist*.[78] Though discrete, the presence of *Geist* in the *Anthropology* is nevertheless decisive. In fact, the brief definition provided does not appear to promise much: "Geist ist das belebende Prinzip im Menschen."* A banal sentence, which, in its trivality, sustains the commonplace expression: "Eine Rede, eine Schrift, eine Dame der Gesellschaft ist schön; aber ohne Geist."** To be attributed with *Geist*, a person has to arouse interest: "*durch Ideen.*"*** A little further on, Kant repeats all these suggestions, knitting them together into a single and enigmatic definition: "Man nennt das durch Ideen belebende Prinzip des Gemüts Geist."****

Let us take our time over the choice of words. We are dealing with a *Prinzip*. Not with a *Vermögen*[79] such as memory, attention, or knowledge in general. Nor with one of those powers (*Kräfte*) which Kant talks about in the Introduction to the *Critique of Judgement*.***** Nor, finally, is this a simple representation like the "I pure" from the first *Critique*. Principle, then: but is it a determining or a regulating principle? Neither the one nor the other, if are to take the "vitalization" that is attributed to it seriously. Might

---

* *Anthropology*, p. 120. ["Spirit is the animating principle in the human being."]

** Ibid., p. 120. ["One says that a speech, a text, a woman in society, etc. are beautiful but without spirit."]

*** Ibid., p. 120. ["By means of *ideas*."]

**** *Anthropology*, p. 142. ["The principle of the mind that animates by means of *ideas* is called spirit."]

***** *Kants Werke*. Cassirer V, p. 189. [*The Critique of Judgement*, op. cit., p. 12: *Kräfte* is translated as "powers."]

there therefore be something in the *Gemüt*—in the way it orients experience, or in its virtual totality—which allies it to life and which has to do with the presence of the *Geist*? Here, a whole new dimension is opened out: the *Gemüt* is not only organized by and armed with the powers and faculties that divide up its domain; the great tripartite structure, which seemed to be given its definitive formulation in the Introduction to the *Critique of Judgement*, did not manage to contain that which, of *Gemüt*, can appear in experience. Like every living being, its lifetime is not indifferently dispersed and scattered; it has its own path to follow; something in it projects it into, without however it being enclosed within, a virtual totality.

In actual fact, we are given no clear indication as to what this principle might consist in. But what it is possible to grasp is how this "vitalization" takes place, the movement by which *Geist* gives the mind the figure of life. "*Durch Ideen*" says the text. What does this mean? How can "the idea of a necessary concept of reason," which Kant understands as "one to which no congruent object can be given in the senses,"* give life to the mind? This could easily be misinterpreted. We might well think that, in its originary temporal dispersion, the *Gemüt* directs itself toward a totalization that would be effected in and by the *Geist*. The *Gemüt* would thus owe its life to this distant, inaccessible, and yet efficient presence. But if that were the case, then the *Geist* would be defined from the outset as a "regulating" principle and not as a "vitalizing" principle. Furthermore, it would mean that the whole thrust of the *Anthropology*

* *Kritik der reinen Vernunft.* Cassirer III, p. 264. [*The Critique of pure Reason*, op. cit., p. 402: "By the idea of a necessary concept of reason, I understand one to which no congruent object can be given in the senses."]

would no longer be tending toward the theme of man living in the world, man as a resident of this cosmopolitical republic with all the duties and rights that are associated with it. Instead, it would be oriented toward the theme of a *Geist* that, little by little, envelops man—and, with him, the world—with its imperious cloak of spiritual sovereignty. It is not the idea of a *Geist* which guarantees the regulation of the empirical diversity of the *Gemüt*, promising it never-ending life.

The "*durch Ideen*" which interests us therefore has another meaning. The important paragraph of the *Critique* entitled: "On the Final Aim of the Natural Dialectic of Human Reason" sheds light on the role that ideas play in the organization of the concrete life of the mind. For it is in effect that, liberated from its transcendental use and the illusions that it cannot help but give rise to, the idea acquires its meaning in the plenitude of experience: there, it anticipates a schema that is not constituting but which opens up the possibility of objects.* It does not reveal the nature of things in an "ostensive" gesture; rather, it gives an advance indication of how nature can be sought.** At last demonstrating that the edge of the universe is beyond the horizon of knowledge, it engages empirical reason in the serious task of an infinite labour.*** In other words, as long as it is experience itself which provides the idea with its field of application, it enters the mind[80] into the mobility of the infinite, endlessly impelling it "to procede still further,"[81] though still managing to avoid losing it in an indepassable dispersion. Thus, empirical reason never reposes idly on the given; and the idea, by

---

* *Kritik der reinen Vernunft.* Cassirer III, p. 459. [*The Critique of pure Reason*, op. cit., p. 607.]

** Ibid., p. 457 [p. 606].

*** Ibid., p. 461 [p. 609].

linking it to the infinite and, at the same time, denying it the infinite, gives it *life* in the realm of the possible. Such then is the function of the *Geist*: it does not organize the *Gemüt* in such a way that it is made it into a living being, or into the analogon of organic life, or indeed into the life of the Absolute itself; rather, its function is to vitalize, to engender, in the passivity of the *Gemüt*, which is that of empirical determination, a teeming mass of ideas—the multiple structures of a totality in the process of becoming that make and unmake themselves like so many of the half-lives that live and die in the mind. Thus the *Gemüt* is not simply "what it is" but "what it makes of itself." And is this not precisely the area of inquiry that the *Anthrolopogy* defines as its field of investigation? To which we only need add that what the *Gemüt* has to make of himself is "the greatest possible empirical use of reason"*—use that is to be the greatest possible thanks to the "*durch Ideen*." The movement which, in the *Critique*, gave rise to the transcendental mirage is extended and prolonged in the *Anthropology* in the form the empirical, concrete life of the *Gemüt*.

From this, a number of consequences arise.

a) The only possible anthropology is that where, rather than being tied to the passivity of phenomenal determinations, the *Gemüt* is instead animated by the work of ideas on the level of the field of experience. The *Geist* is therefore the principle, in the *Gemüt*, of a de-dialecticized, nontranscendental dialectic oriented toward the domain of experience and playing an integral part in the play of phenomena itself. It is the *Geist* which offers the *Gemüt* the freedom of the possible, stripping it of its determinations, and providing it with a future which it owes to nothing but itself.

---

* *Kritik der reinen Vernunft*. Cassirer. III. p. 461. [*Critique of pure reason*, op. cit., p. 609.]

b) We now understand that anthropology renders an empirical psychology impossible, as well as a knowledge of the mind[82] that could be developed entirely on the level of nature. Without the "*belebendes Prinzip*," it would only ever have access to a mind that is asleep, inert, dead—which would make it a "physiology" minus the life. The Preface to the 1798 text attests to this: the possibility of a nonpragmatic anthropology is acknowledged in theory, as having a place within the general system of knowledge of man. But while it is announced in the name of a structural symmetry, as a content of knowledge it is rejected: the study of memory as a simple fact of nature is not only futile, it is impossible: "All theoretical speculation about this is a pure waste of time."* The presence of the *Geist* and, with it, this dimension of freedom and of totality which transcends the *Gemüt*, ensure that the only true anthropology is a pragmatic anthropology, where each fact is placed within the open system of *Können* and *Sollen*. And Kant only wrote one kind.

c) Given these conditions, might not the *Geist* have something to do with this enigmatic "nature of our reason,"** which is also in question in the *Dialectic* and the *Methodology* of *Pure Reason*? An unsettling notion. The movement of the *Critique*, having reached its summit, would seem to be sent abruptly back in the direction of the empirical, toward a realm of facts where man would be entirely given over to the most originary form of passivity. All of a sudden, the transcendental would be relieved of its duties, and the conditions of experience finally be brought back to the originary inertia

---

* *Anthropology*, Preface, p. 3.

** *Kritil der reinen Vernunft*. Cassirer. III. p. 456 and p. 536. [The reference mark to this footnote is not indicated in the text, but in all likelihood it refers to this point. See *The Critique of Pure Reason*, op. cit., p. 605 and p. 673.]

of a nature. But does this "nature of our reason" play the same role here as the nature of human understanding in Hume, that of the first explanation and the final reduction? For the moment, let us simply note a structural analogy between this "nature" that urges reason "to venture to the outermost bounds of all cognition by means of mere ideas in a pure use,"* without itself containing "original deceptions and semblances"** (is this not, after all, nature pure and simple?), and the concrete life of the mind as it is described in the *Anthropology*. For it, too, is animated by a spontaneous movement which repeatedly exposes it to the danger of being played by its own game, but which is always played in an initial innocence. Both are always on the point of losing, and breaking free from, themselves but in their proper movement remain nevertheless, "the highest court of appeal for all rights and claims."***

d) If this analogy is well-founded, we are justified in asking whether the *Geist*, which emerges within the confines of anthropological reflection, is in fact secretly indispensable to the structure of Kantian thought; something like the seed of pure reason, the deep-rooted origin of its transcendental illusions, the infallible judge of its return to its legitimate domain, the principle of its movement within the empirical field where the faces of truth ceaselessly appear one after another. The *Geist* would be that originary fact which, in its transcendental version, implies that the infinite is never present, but always in an essential retreat; and, in its empirical version, that the infinite is what animates the movement toward truth and as the endless succession of its forms. The

---

* Ibid., p. 536. [*The Critique of Pure Reason*, op. cit., p. 673.]

** Ibid., p. 456. [*The Critique of Pure Reason*, op. cit., p. 605.]

*** Ibid., p. 456. [Ibid.]

Geist is at the root of the possibility of knowledge. And, because of this, it is indissociably present and absent in the figures of knowledge: it is this retreat, this invisible and "visible reserve" and it is in its inaccessible distance that knowledge takes its place and acquires its positivity. Its mode of being is being not there; in precisely this, it outlines the place of truth.

The unique and sovereign structure of this originary fact gives the *necessity* of critical thinking and the *possibility* of *Anthropology*.

What connections between these two modes of thought warrant this radical element which appears to be common to both?

Such is the difference in level between the *Critique* and the *Anthropology* that it initially discourages a structural comparison between the two. A collection of empirical observations, anthropology is not "in contact" with a philosophy of the conditions of experience. And yet this essential difference is not of the order of a nonrelation. A certain inverted analogy casts the *Anthropology* as the negative of the *Critique*.

a) In the *Anthropology*, the relationships between synthesis and the given are the mirror-image of how they appear in the *Critique*.

Consider subjectivity, for example. As regards anthropology, Kant spent a long time hestitating over this point. The texts from the 70–80 period link the expression of the 'I' to the possibility of being an object for oneself.* But it is not clear whether it is the 'I' itself that is at the root of this possibility, or if it is rooted in the objectification that this possibility enables. The *Critique*, for its part, comes to a decision: the 'I' can never be the object, only the

---

* *Kants Schriften.* XV, 2, p. 661. [In *AA*.]

form of the synthesis. Now, in the 1798 text, when the 'I' is considered in its fundamental synthetic function, it also assumes the simple status of an object. It appears, abruptly assuming a fixed form that from then on remains constant in the field of experience. The impact of the spoken 'I' marks the passage from sentiment to thought—from *Fühlen* to *Denken*. Without being the agent or simply the conscious awareness of this passage, it is the empirical and manifest form in which the synthetic activity of the 'I' appears as a figure already synthesised—a structure that is at once first and second: it is not given to man from the beginning, as a kind of a priori of existence; but when it does appear, inscribing itself within the multiplicity of a chronicle of sensations, it presents itself as already having been there, like the irreducible content of a thought which can operate only once that figure of experience is constituted: it is in this 'I' that the subject will become aware of its past and carry out the synthesis of its identity. Put another way, the *a priori of knowledge* from the point of view of the *Critique* cannot immediately be transposed into the *a priori of existence* in the terms of the anthropology; it appears in the density of a becoming where its sudden emergence infallibly assumes the retrospectively constituted meaning of the already there.

The structure is inverted for the originary dispersion of the given. From an anthropological perspective, the given is, in effect, never offered on the basis of an inert multiplicity that is the decisive indication of an originary passivity, and which appeals to the synthetic activity of consciousness in all of its diverse forms. The dispersion of the given is always already reduced in *Anthropology*, secretly dominated by a whole variety of syntheses operated outside of the visible work of consciousness: it is the unconscious syntheses of the elements of perception and obscure representations that

even the light of our understanding is not always capable of disso-
ciating;* these are the schemas of exploration that trace, in space,
little islands of synthesis;** in sensibility, these reorganizations are
what permit the subsitution of one sense for another;*** these are
the strengthenings and the weakenings of the sensible effects which
anticipate, as it were spontaneously, the voluntary syntheses of
attention.**** Thus, what in the *Critique* was welcomed as the infinitely thin surface of a multiplicity which has nothing in common
with itself other than being originarily given, is shown, in *Anthropology*, in the light of an unexpected depth: as already grouped and
organized, as having already been given the provisional or solid figures of synthesis. That which, for consciousness, is the pure given,
does not present itself as such in concrete existence. For an anthropology, absolutely originary passivity is never there.

Thus, the structure of the relationship between the given and
the a priori in *Anthropology* is the opposite of that revealed in the
Critique. The a priori, in the order of knowledge, becomes, in the
order of concrete existence, an *originary* which is not chronologi-
cally first, but which, having appeared in the succession of figures
of the synthesis, reveals itself as already there; on the other hand,
that which, in the order of knowledge, is a pure given, is, in the
reflection on concrete existence, lit up by muted lights which give
it the depth of the already occured.

b) *Anthropology* maintains the division of the "faculties"—*Vermögen*—as in the *Critique*. However, its privileged domain is not

---

* *Anthropology*, p. 25.

** Ibid., p. 46.

*** Ibid., p. 51.

**** Ibid., p. 55.

that where the faculties and powers show off their positive attributes but where they show their failings—or at least where they face danger, where they risk being obliterated. Rather than their nature or the full form of their activity, anthropology is concerned with pointing up the movement by which the faculties, distancing themselves from their center and their justification, become other than themselves, illegitimate. In line with its fundamentally propedeutical aim, no doubt the *Critique* sought to denounce and to dismantle the transcendental use of reason simply by constantly referring to the positive aspects of each *Vermögen*. In anthropological investigation, however, the pursuit of each faculty takes the path of all possible deviation. Self-awareness, for example, is defined not as a form of experience and the condition of a limited but grounded knowledge; instead, it looks more like the always resurgent temptation of a polymorphous egoism: the possibility of saying 'I' gives consciousness the allure of a "beloved Me" which fascinates it to the extent that, in a paradoxical return, it renounces the language of the first person—as decisive as it had nevertheless been—so as to reproduce itself in the fiction of an 'Us.'* The study of sensibility, while repeating the great critical opposition between *Schein*[83] and *Erscheinung*,[84] does not investigate what grounds this phenomenon; instead, it explores that which is at once fascinating and precarious in the dazzle of appearance: how it veils what it makes sparkle, and at what point it happens to convey what it unveils.** The extended analysis of the deficiencies and illnesses of the mind prompts a brief paragraph on reason; and we only have to look at how mental pathology is accorded increasing importance in the notes and the

---

* *Anthropology*, p. 18.

** Ibid., p. 40–41.

other projects that led up to the fully developed 1798* text to see how these reflections on negativity were moving in the same direction as the anthropological research. To critical thought, which represents the investigation into that which is *conditional* in the *founding* activity, *Anthropology* responds by offering an inventory of what is *un-founded* in the *conditioned*. In the anthropological domain, there is no synthesis that it is not under threat: it is as if the realm of experience were hollowed out from within by dangers which are not of the order of some arbitrary going beyond, but of collapse.

Possible experience, in its limited range, defines the field of the loss of truth with as much success as it does the field of truth.

c) At last, a detail acquires its significance. All the *Collegentwürfe* and the—fairly late—text published by Starke give the general plan of the *Anthropology* as divided into two parts: an *Elementarlehre* and a *Methodenlehre*. The 1798 text is in effect divided into two sections, but one is a *Didactic* and the other a *Characteristic*. This change, which was no doubt made in the years leading up to the publication of the book, is all the more surprising given that the content and the order do not seem to have undergone any modification whatsoever. The distinction between a doctrine of the elements and a doctrine of the method is in keeping with the critical research: on the one hand, that which constitutes the faculty of knowledge, and on the other, that which governs its exercise in the realm of possible experience. Apparently, the *Anthropology* is built on the same model: first come the diverse "faculties," the organization of which forms the totality of the *Gemüt* (the *Elementarlehre*); then, the rules governing their exercise for an individual, a family, within a population or a race, and

---

* Ibid., p. 96–114.

at the heart of humanity (the *Methodenlehre*). But this is merely a *trompe l'oeil*—an adjustement to the norms of the *Critique* which was not in keeping with the vocation of the text.

The terms *Didactic* and *Characteristic* which appear at the very last stage of reflection, and which are therefore the substitutes for the traditional distinction, are accompanied by curious subtitles whose relationship to the titles is difficult to fathom. For the *Didactic* it is a question of "the Way of Cognizing the Interior as Well as the Exterior of the Human Being,"[85] and for the *Characteristic*, "the Way of cognizing the Interior of the Human Being from the Exterior." Is this change a reorganization of the whole, a move away from critical thought? No, indubitably. Rather, it is the discovery of that which was already, obscurely, and prior to any explanation, the thematic of the *Anthropology*: that is, the direct coordination which ensures that research into the field of the *Gemüt* leads to an interior knowledge of the self, but also that it overflows spontaneously, and without recourse to the limit or any further extrapolation into the knowledge of man in the exterior forms by which he is manifested. For as long as the term *Elementarlehre* was imposed by the symmetry of the *Critique*, the analysis of the *Gemüt* could only make sense of itself under the auspices of an investigation into the powers in the virtuality of the Vermögen, and at the root of the possible. But, once it was free to assume its true meaning, that investigation knew that, by concerning itself with the interior, it engages with the exterior at the same time; that man does not make anything of his possibilities without also being engaged in their manifestations. What the *Critique* discerned as the possible in the order of the conditions (*Vermögen*) and the real in the order of the constituted (*Erscheinung*) is given in *Anthropology* as an indivisable continuity: the secret of Power reveals itself in the dazzle of the Phenomenon, where it finds both its truth and the truth of its perversion (when use becomes abuse, as in the language of the first person); and Power, in its perversion, is denounced by the Phenomenon, which then imperiously calls Power back to this radical truth which links Power to itself in the mode of obligation. It is this that gives each paragraph of the First Part its obscure three-beat rhythm: Power at the root of its possibilities; Power found then lost, translated and betrayed in its Phenomenon; Power linked imperatively to itself. So, for example: self-consciousness, egoism, the effective consciousness of representations; or, imagination as the power of originary "invention," imagination in the fantastical shipwreck of the dream, imagination in poetry linked to the sign. Or, again: the power to desire with one's emotions; the false truth of the passions; the place of sovereign good. What links the *Vermögen* to the *Erscheinung* is both of the order of a manifestation, of venturing as far as perdition, and of an ethical bond. There, precisely, lies the articulation of the *Können* and the *Sollen* which, as we have seen, is indispensable to anthropological thought. The art of knowing the interior as well as the exterior of man is therefore not, strictly speaking, a theory of elements but a *Didactic*: it does not *discover* without *teaching* and *prescribing*. As for the *Characteristic*, it shows that the ensembles of phenonema—the body, the couple, the race, the species—are not closed in upon themselves, given once and for all, but are what relates the apparently immobile truths of phenomena back to those radical possibilities that gave them meaning and movement; it allows us to go from the sign back to the power, "*das Innere des Menschen aus dem Äusseren zu erkennen.*"[86]

The critical model, having imposed itself for so long, is succeeded by an articulation which repeats it, but as in a negative:

the theory of the elements becomes a prescription with respect to all possible phenomena (which, strictly speaking, was the goal of the *Methodenlehre*).[87] Conversely, the theory of the method becomes a regressive analysis that aims to uncover to the primitive seed of the powers (which was the intention of the *Elementarlehre*).[88] A repetition, then, but back-to-front, as in a mirror. This is how close, and, at the same time, how distant the region where the a priori of knowledge is defined is from the domain specifying the a prioris of existence. That which is announced in the order of conditions appears, in the form of the originary, as both same and other.

If this distant proximity is to be seen more clearly, it is all the more urgent that we discover what relationship the *Anthropology* bears to the *Critique*.

Two texts are of singular importance: a passage from the *Transcendental Method*, to which we have already referred with regard to psychology; and a fairly enigmatic piece of evidence from the *Logic*.

1) *The Architectonics of Pure Reason*. Pure philosophy (in which, as a propedeutics, the *Critique* is included), makes no room for anthropology. "Rational physiology," which thinks of Nature as the *Inbegriff aller Gegenstände der Sinne* knows only physics and rational psychology. On the other hand, in the vast field of empirical philosophy, two domains balance each other out: that of physics, and that of an anthropology whose task it is to take in the smaller edifice of an empirical psychology.

At first glance, there appears to be no rigorous symmetry between pure philosophy and empirical philosophy. The correspondence that is immediately evident with regard to physics stops short when it is a question of inner sense and the human being. Unlike psychology, anthropology is only ever on the side of empirical philosophy; it cannot therefore be governed or controlled by the *Critique*, inasmuch as the latter is concerned with pure reason. No more than the construction of Newtonian physics required or needed to be verified by critical philosophy, *Anthropology*, taking up the place set aside for it by the *Architectonic*, has no need of a preliminary critique. Hence, there is no possibility of the *Critique* holding any sway over the form or the content of the *Anthropology*. Between the one kind of thinking and the other, there is no contact whatsoever. Is not all of this in any case confirmed (negatively) by the *Anthropology* itself? At no point is the *Critique* invoked: the correspondences between the two texts might be easy to discern, but at no point are they given or conceived as such. It is buried inside the text of Anthropology, serving as its framework, and it should be envisaged in this way: as a structural fact, not as the manifestation of a preconceived and intentional plan.

2) *The Logic.* We are familiar with the three fundamental questions enumerated in the *Transcendental Method*: What can I know?—a speculative question to which the *Critique* responds "that which reason ought to be satisfied with"; What should I do?—a practical question; What may I hope for?—a question that is at once theoretical and practical. Now, these three questions which hang over and, up to a certain point, dictate the organization of the *Critique*, reappear at the beginning of the *Logic*, but having undergone a decisive change. A fourth question is added: What is man?—a question which follows on from the first three only to gather them together in a single frame of reference: for *all*

of the questions must come ultimately down to this, as must anthropology, metaphysics, morality and religion.*

Is this sudden movement, which reorients the first three questions, pointing them in the direction of anthropology, the sign of a rupture in Kant's thinking? The *Philosophieren* seems to be entirely engaged on the level of the knowledge of man; the important empirical status that the first *Critique* assigned to *Anthropology* is, therefore, challenged—this is no longer the last empirical degree of a philosophically organized knowledge, but the point at which philosophical reflection culminates in an interrogation of the questions themselves. But we should be careful not to rush either into condemning a supposed rupture impacting on the transcendental resolution of criticism, or into celebrating the discovery of a hypothetical new dimension through which Kant would finally approach what was, originarily, closest to him.

First of all, what does it mean for the three questions to "relate to the fourth" (*sich beziehen auf*)? Are we to understand that relationship in terms of that between knowledge and the object, or that same knowledge and the subject—if, as a text from the *Logic* still has it, knowledge has "*eine zwiefache Beziehung: erstlich, eine Beziehung auf das Objekt, zweites eine Beziehung auf das Subjekt.*"**[89] In other words, are we to understand that, in these three questions, man was the obscure "*Gegenstand*"—they opened onto him, and he stood before them, poised to provide the unexpected response they had been solliciting in another language? Or, on the contrary, is it that these

---

* Logik, Cassirer VII. pp. 343–344. [In fact, the reference is to *Kants Werke*, edited by Cassirer, op. cit., vol. VIII. But see also *AA*, vol. IX: "What can I know? What should I do? What may I hope for? What is a human being? The first question is answered in *metaphysics*, the second in *morals*, the third in *religion*, and the fourth in *anthropology*," p. 25.]
** Ibid., p. 350. [*AA*, vol. IX, p. 33.]

three questions must in turn be interrogated, their questioning power turned back on itself and restored, by way of a new Copernican revolution, to an originary gravitation around man, who naturally believes that he is being questioned, when all the while it is he who is asking the questions, which involves doing away with all philodoxy and asking the questions *with regard* to himself. Let us begin our investigation by noting that the *Anthrolopology* as we know it does not at any point present itself as a response to the fourth question, nor even as the greatest empirical exploitation of this very question; in fact, that question is asked much later, in another context, from a point of view that is not properly anthropological, and only once the organization of the *Philosophieren* in Kantian thought is complete— which is to say, in the *Logic* and in the *Opus Postumum*.

It is in the light of the answers provided in these texts to *Was ist der Mensch?* that, working backwards, we will try to understand the meaning of *Anthropology*.

The texts of the *Opus Postumum* which date from the period 1800–1 endlessly repeat the question of how, with regard to the division of transcendental philosophy, to define the relations between God, world, and man. And what might look to us like a rupture or a discovery in the *Logic*, now shows itself to be the fundamental question of philosophical reflection, taken up again both in the rigour of its limitations and in its widest possible sense. This point is made in one of the fragments: *"System der Transc. Philosophie in drei Abschnitten: Gott, die Welt, universum, und Ich selbst der Mensch als moralisches Wesen."**

---

* *Kants Schriften*, Ak. XXI., p. 27 [See I. Kant, *Opus Postumum*, edited, with an Introduction and Notes, by Eckart Förster, translated by Eckart Förster and Michael Rosen, Cambridge University Press, Cambridge: 1993, p. 231: "System of Transcendental Philosophy in Three Sections. God, the *world*, universum, and I myself, man, as moral being."]

But these three notions are not given as the three elements of a planned system that would juxtapose them on a basis of a homogenous plane. The third term is not there as a complement, a third part in the organization of the whole; rather, it plays the central role as a "*Medius terminus.*"* It is the concrete and active unit in which and by which God and the world acquire their own, respective unity: "*Gott, die Welt, und der Mensch als Person, d.i. als Wesen das diese Begriffe vereinigt.*"** We should allow the fragments that make up the *Opus Postumum* their exploratory character and, in the obsessive repetition of the same themes, listen out for this divergence which is at one with the originary unity of the undertaking. This *Vereinigung* of God and of the world in man and by man—what does it really mean? What synthesis or operation is it aiming at? On what level can it be situated: the empirical or the transcendental, the originary or the fundamental?

a) Some texts refer to it as the very act of thinking. If man gives unity to the world and to God, it is in the sense that he exercises his sovereignity as a thinking subject—thinking the world and thinking God: "*Der medius terminus... ist hier das urteilende Subjekt (das denkende Welt Wesen, der Mensch...).*"***

b) This act of unification is therefore the synthesis of thought itself. But it can, in precisely this sense, be defined on the basis of the power from which it originates: "*Gott und die Welt, und der Geist des Menschen der beide denkt*";**** or be just as well considered

---

* Ibid., p. 27.

** Ibid., p. 29. [*Opus Postumum*, op. cit.: "God, the world, and man as a person: that is, as a being who unites these concepts," p. 233.]

*** Ibid., p. 27. [*Opus Postumum*, op. cit.: "The *medius terminus* (copula) ... is here the judging subject (the thinking world-being, man...)," p. 231.]

**** Ibid., p. 29. [*Opus Postumum*, op. cit.: "God and the world, and the human mind which thinks both," p. 233.]

in its single form, as if God, the world and man, in their co-exis-tence and their fundamental relations, put the very structure of judgement back under the regime of traditional Logic; the trilogy *Subjekt, Praedikat, Copula* defines the form of what relates God, the world and man. It is therefore the copula, the link—like the verb 'to be' in the judgement of the universe.

c) At last man emerges as universal synthesis, forming a real unity in which the personality of God and the objectivity of the world are rejoined, the sensible principle and the *supra* sensible; and man becomes the mediatory from which "*ein absoluter Ganze*"* takes shape. It is from the starting point of man that the absolute can be thought.

Responses—or solutions? These texts should not be read as either the one or the other. Rather, as possible, and tested, paths for a mode of thinking advancing across the ground of a transcenden-tal philosophy at last regained. And, at each point, so as to get the bearings of this new territory, the question of man arises, as if it were the question to which every problematic of the world and of God cannot help but be related.

But this relation to the question of man does not have the value of an absolute reference—which would free up a serenely fundamental thinking. The very content of the question *Was ist der Mensch?* cannot inhere in an originary autonomy, for man immediately defines himself as a citizen of the world, as "*Weltbe-wohner*":** "*Der Mensch gehört zwar mit zur Welt.*"*** And,

---

* Ibid., p. 31. [*Opus Postumum*, op. cit.: "an absolute whole," p. 234.]

** Ibid., p. 27. [*Opus Postumum*, op. cit.: "inhabitant of the world," p. 231.]

*** Ibid., p. 38. [Not translated in the English edition: "The human being belongs to the world."]

completing the circle, all reflection on man involves reflection on the world. However, at issue here is not the naturalist perspective where a science of man implies a knowledge of nature. What is in question are not the determinations, on the level of phenomena, in which the human animal is caught and defined; rather, it is the development of self-awareness and of the 'I am': the subject self-affecting by the movement in which he becomes aware of himself as an object: "Ich bin.—Es ist eine Welt ausser mir (*praeter me*) im Raume und der Zeit, und ich bin selbst ein Weltwesen; bin mir jenes Verhältnisses bewusst[90] und der bewegenden Kräfte zu Empfindungen (Wahrnehmungen).—Ich der Mensch bin mir selbst ein äusseres Sinnenobjekt, ein Teil de Welt."* It is in the implications of 'I am' that the world is discovered—as the figure of this movement through which the self, in becoming an object, takes its place in the field of experience and finds there a concrete system of belonging. The world thus revealed is therefore not the *Physis*, nor the realm of the validity of laws. And, in fact, while the discovery of this world just so happened to be anticipated and made possible by the *Transcendental Analytic* and the *Refutation of Idealism*, it is not exactly this world—or rather, it is not the world in the same sense—that is in question in the fragment of the *Opus Postumum*. The "exterior things" of the *Refutation of Idealism* were the condition of the determination of time as a form of inner experience: the world of the *Opus Postumum* is the concomitant of the determination of the self as the objective

---

* Ibid., p. 63. [Not translated in the English edition. "I am.—There is a world outside of me, in space and in time, and I am a earthly being myself; I am aware of this relation and of the changing powers of sensations. I, the human being, am a sensible object to myself, a part of the world."]

content of experience in general. And rather than being defined by "persistence," the "obstination" (*Beharrliches*) of a spatial coexistence, it emerges in the curve of a whole which means, for the experience of the self, it serves more as a blanket covering than a landmark. It is no longer the correlative of a *Zeitbestimmung*, but the presupposition of a *Sinnenbestimmung* of the self. It is not given in the ouverture of the *All*; it is present in the curve of the *Ganz* inclining back toward itself.*

It is not easy to speak of this world. Its realization in the curve which contains it seems to exclude it from language, and from its initial form which is that of a prediction: a text in the *Opus Postumum* speaks of "personality" as being the predicate of God; but it stumbles over that which, for the sake of symmetry, ought to be the predicate of the world. This predicate remains a blank, beyond language, because the world, as a whole (*Ganz*), is beyond all predication and is perhaps even at the root of all predicates. And yet the world is not without structure or meaning. Its opposition to the universe determines its meaning in a transcendental philosophy.

1) Unlike the universe, the world is given in a system of actuality which envelops all real existence. It envelops that existence both because the world is the concept of its totality, and because all existence develops its concrete reality on the basis of the world. This double meaning is implied in the word *Inbegriff*: "*Der Begriff der Welt ist der Inbegriff des Daseins.*"** The world is the root of existence, the *source*, which, *containing* existence, manages both to *retain* it and to *set it free*.

---

* *Kants Schriften*. Ak. XXI. p. 22. [Section not translated in the English edition. "Whole"].

** Ibid., p. 36. [*Opus Postumum*, op. cit., "The concept of the world is the complex of the existence," p. 238.]

2) By definition, there can only be one universe. On the other hand, though, there could be a number of different worlds (*"es mag viele Welte sein"*). The universe is the unity of the possible, while the world is the system of real relations. Once this system is given, there is no question of those relations being otherwise; that said, there is nothing to prevent us conceiving of *another* system where *other* relations might be *differently* defined.* Which is to say that the world is not the open space of the necessary, but a *domain* in which a system of necessity is possible.

3) But, to allow for such speculation (*"es mag…"*), it first has to be acknowledged that there can only ever be one world: *"Es mag*[91] *nur Eine Welt sein."*** For the possible is thinkable only from within a given system of actuality, and the plurality of worlds is only ever seen from the standpoint of the existing world and whatever available experience we have of it: the world is *"the Ganze aller möglichen Sinnen Gegenständen."* *** The corollary of the possibility of conceiving of other worlds—this one being, *de facto*, only a domain—is the impossibility of moving beyond the world we inhabit and the imperious necessity of accepting its *frontiers* as *limits*. Thus the world, once again taken to mean the *"Inbegriff des Daseins,"* appears on the basis of the three-way structure, in keeping with the *Begriff des Inbegriffs*, of *source*, *domain*, and *limit*. Such, according to the *Opus Postumum*, is the world in which man appears to himself.

---

* Ibid., p. 30. [*Opus Postumum*, op. cit., pp. 233–234.]

** Ibid., p. 30. [*Opus Postumum*, op. cit.: "Taken in this sense there can, thus, only be one world," p. 234.]

*** Ibid., p. 31. [*Opus Postumum*, op. cit.: *"The world…* is the whole of sense-objects," p. 234. In the German version we read: "Die Welt… heisst das Ganze der Sinnengegenstande," p. 31.]

Now, let us return to the *Logic*, taking up the thread at the point where we left off, the moment when the three questions were referred back to the fourth. What is man? For its part, this question does not remain stable in the face of, nor is it closed off from, the void that it defines and interrogates. As soon as it is formulated, the *Was ist der Mensch?* gives rise to three further questions—or, rather, to the formulation of three imperatives of knowledge which together give the anthropological question its character of a concrete prescription: "Der Philosoph muss also bestimmen können:

1. Die Quellen des menschlichen Wissens

2. Der Umfang des möglichen und natürlichen Gebrauches alles Wissens

3. Und endlich die Grenzen die Vernunft."*

The question of man is shared between these three prescriptions; what do they mean, and to what do they refer? It is not hard to find, implicit in these three themes, both the repetition of the first three questions and the sketch of what in the *Opus Postumum* will become the basic structure of the "*Inbegriff des Daseins.*" On the one hand, establishing "the sources of human knowledge" effectively gives the content of the question "What can I know?"; determining the "domain of the natural and possible use of knowledge" indicates what a possible response to the question "What should I do?" might be; and establishing the "limits of reason" gives meaning to that which "one may hope for."

---

* Logik. Cassirer. VIII, p. 344. [In *AA*, p. 25: "The Philosopher must also be able to determine: 1. The sources of human knowledge. 2. The extent of the possible and natural use of every knowledge. 3. finally, the limits of reason."]

Once the content of the fourth question has been specified, we see that it is not fundamentally different to the meaning of the first three. Moreover relating to theses three to the last does not mean that they will be dissolved by it, nor that they refer to a new question which goes beyond them; it simply means that the anthropological question *asks*, by repeating them, the questions that relate to it. We are at the level of the structural foundation of the *anthropologico-critical repetition*. The *Anthropology* says nothing *other* than what is said in the *Critique*; we need only glance through the 1798 text to see that it covers exactly the same ground as the critical enterprise.

However, the meaning of this fundamental repetition must not be asked of the words that are repeated nor of the language that repeats, but instead of that toward which the repetition is directed. Which is to say, of the revelation of that three-beat structure which is in question in the *Opus Postumum* and which characterises the *Inbegriff das Daseins*: source, domain, limit. These concepts are common to the themes that specify the fourth question in the *Logic*, as well as to those which, in Kant's last texts, give meaning to the notion of the world as a whole. These are the concepts which determine the structural connection between the question of man and the world called into question. And this, through the rigorous repetition of the three questions that had governed the three *Critiques*. In other words, these three notions, *Quellen*, *Umfang*, and *Grenzen*, already present in the fabric of critical thought, manage, thanks to their perserverance and their proper weightiness, to reach that fundamental level where the *Inbegriff* of existence is interrogated and where they at last appear in their own right. On the most superficial level, they present themselves as the common forms of both the question of man and of the meaning of the world. On that level of transcendental philosophy, though, they no doubt have quite another significance.

"*Was notwendig (ursprünglich) das Dasein der Dingen ausmacht gehört zur Transc. Philosophie.*"* Now, what belongs necessarily (originarily) to the existence of things is the foundational structure of its *Inbegriff* that we are already familiar with. The richness of the source, the solidity of the domain, the rigour of the frontier all belong to what is necessary (that is to say, originary) for all existence conceived as *Ganz*[92] and not as *All*.[93] And it is in this way that the connection between man and the world is revealed in its most fundamental form—this connection which appeared to be caught in an infinite repetition of a circularity: because man gives unity to the world, himself nothing more than a citizen of the world. Does not a text from the *Opus Postumum* say that "*Der Mensch in der Welt gehört mit zur Kenntniss der Welt?*"**

But these are paradoxes only on the level of natural knowledge. On the level of a transcendental philosophy, they quickly dissolve, making way for a correlation where the whole of existence defines what belongs to it necessarily and originarily.

1) The world, as *source* of knowledge, is given in those forms of multiplicity that designate the originary passivity of sensibility; but the world is precisely the inexhaustible *source* of knowledge in the sense that this originary passivity is indissociable from the forms of the *Vereinigung* and the spontaneity of the mind. If the world is *source*, it is because there is a fundamental correlation, beyond which we cannot go back any further, between passivity and spontaneity.

---

* *Kants Schriften*. Ak. XXI, p. 7. [In *AA*: "what necessarily (originally) determines the existence of things belongs to transcendental philosophy."]

** Ibid., p. 61. [In *AA*, XXI: "The human being in the world is part of the knowledge of the world."]

2) As the *domain* of all possible predicates, the world is given as bound up with a determinism which relates to the a priori syntheses of the judging subject ("*eines urteilenden Subjekts*").[94] And because of precisely this, the world is a domain only in relation to a founding activity which initiates freedom; in consequence of which "*der Mensch gehört zwar mit zur Welt, aber nicht der seiner Pflicht Angemessene.*"*

3) As the *limit* of possible experience, the world excludes all transcendental use of the idea. But it is a *limit* only because a certain "nature" of reason exists whose work it is to anticipate the totality, and think of it precisely as a limit, because the very ambiguity of this notion is to designate both the frontier too easily crossed and that inaccessible term that we always approaching, but never actually go beyond. Ambiguity which is expressed in this fragment: "*Gott über mir, die Welt ausser mir, der Menschliche Geist in mir in einem System das All der Dinge befassend....*"**

We see the expanse of the field of reflection that these three notions—source, domain, limit—cover. In a sense, they correspond to the trilogy, internal to the first *Critique*, of sensibility, understanding, and reason. Further on, they rehearse and summarise the work of each *Critique* in a single word: pure reason, practical reason, faculty of judgement. They repeat the three fundamental questions that, according to Kant, aminate all the *Philosphieren*. They at last provide the question of man (to which all the other questions related) with a three-fold content. But, taking

---

* Ibid., p. 38. ["The human being is part of the world, but only to the extent that he fulfils his duty fully"; Kant says: "[...] *aber nicht der seiner* ganzen *Pflicht angemessene.*" (emphasis mine)].

** Ibid., p. 39. ["God above me, the world outside of me, the human mind inside of me, in a system which encompasses the totality of things."]

up each of the tripartitions again this way, they are made to reach, by way of their very repetition, the fundamental level, and the systematic divisions between them are replaced by their transcendental equivalents. Thus it becomes clear that the world is not simply source for a sensible 'faculty,' but the basis of the transcendental correlation of passivity-spontaneity; that the world is not simply domain for a synthetic understanding, but the basis of the transcendental correlation necessity-liberty; that the world does not simply impose a limit on the use of Ideas, but is the basis of the transcendental correlation reason-mind (*Vernunft-Geist*). And, in this way, this system of correlations serves as the basis for the reciprocal transcendence of truth and freedom.

We see what place is given to the fourth question in the economy of the final episode of Kantian thought, which is to say in the passage from a critical—hence necessarily propedeutic—reflection to the realization of a transcendental philosophy. The anthropological question has no independent content of its own; it repeats the first three questions, but it repeats them by substituting a tripartition that was more or less directly lifted from the division of the faculties (*Vermögen*) with the play of the three notions that cover the whole field of connections between man and the world. Not empirical and circular connections between immanences on the level of natural knowledge, but the necessary—that is to say, the originary, *notwendig (ursprünglich)*—correlations from which, from the root of the existence of things, inseparable transcendences emerged.

The meaning and function of the question *What is man?* is to carry the divisions of the *Critique* to the level of a fundamental cohesion: that of a structure, more radical than any possible "faculty" lends itself to transcendental philosophy, liberated at last.

And yet we have not reached the end of the road. Or rather, we have already gone too far down the path which was supposed to lead us the exact position of *Anthropology*—to its birth-place and to the moment it inserted itself into critical thought. As if an anthropology only looked possible (not only its programmatic but also its fundamental possibility) from the standpoint of the *Critique* having already reached its end, having already led to the realization of transcendental philosophy. But there is still further to go: the question "What is man?" presents itself in the *Logic* as the anthropological question par excellence. And yet, in the *Opus Postumum*, it is linked, from the very beginning, to the interrogation of God and the world; the question is fully developed on this level, as if it had nothing to do with the singular domain that is anthropology. The reference in the *Logic* to an anthropology that would bring all philosophical interrogation back to itself appears to have been no more than a fleeting episode in Kantian thought. An episode situated between an anthropology that has no pretensions to such universal meaning, and a transcendental philosophy which takes the question of man to another, far more radical level. This episode was structurally necessary: its transcient character is linked to the transition that it made possible.

The relationship between the 1798 text and the *Critique* is therefore paradoxical. On the one hand, the *Critique* announces and makes space for anthropology at the heart of an empirical philosophy; the *Anthropology*, for its part, makes no reference to the *Critique* or to the organizing principles that it sets out. On the other hand, the *Anthropology* repeats the general articulations of the *Critique*, as well as the now traditional division of the faculties, as if it went without saying that it should do so; and yet, despite this implict and constant reference to the *Critique*, the latter has no foundational value with regard to the *Anthropology*. The *Anthropology* rests on the *Critique* but is not rooted in it. It inclines spontaneously toward that which must serve as its foundation: not critical, but transcendental philosophy itself. It is there that we will discover the structure and the function of its empiricity.

We must now pursue this empiricity for its own sake. From what we have managed to glimpse of the direction in which it is heading, doubtless this question will help us to better understand how *Anthropology* could have been marginal with regard to the *Critique* and yet decisive for the forms of reflection that came after it.

The Anthropology describes itself as both "systematic and popular"; and it is by unpacking these two words that we will be able to decipher its true meaning: to repeat the *Critique* on the 'popular' level of advice, narrative and example, and so to secretly set Kantian thought on the path toward a founding philosophy.

1) The Anthropology is systematic. This does not mean that it states everything one could possibly know about man but that, as knowledge, it forms a coherent whole: not a *Alles* but *ein Ganzes*.[95] Now, the principle of this totality is not man himself, taken as an already coherent object because he is linked to the world. Only the undefined work of investigation and frequentation (*Umgang*) can find out what he is. If the Anthropology is systematic it is in the sense that it borrows its coherence from the whole of the critical enterprise: the three books of the *Didactic* repeat those of the three *Critiques*, while the *Characteristic* reproduces the texts on history, the future of humanity and its progress towards unknowable ends. In this, and only this, resides the organizing principle of anthropology.

An example will show precisely how this repetition works. The text entitled *Apology for Sensibility** repeats the connections between

---

* *Anthropology*, p. 34 and ff.

intuition and understanding. But this repetition is not a return to the same. The relationship described by *Anthropology* has its proper dimension in the slow, precarious and always doubtful work of succession: multiplicity, as it is given to the senses, is not yet (*noch nicht*) ordered; in addition, understanding is required (*hinzukommen*), which must instate the order it brings (*hineinbringen*). A judgement reached in advance of this ordering (*zuvor*) risks being false. On the other hand, this sequence cannot be extended indefinitely; with time, the retrospective mulling over of reasoning (*Nachgrübeln*) and the vague movement of reflection (*Überlegung*) may intervene, but error can creep in at this stage too. The given is therefore never deceptive, not because man judges well, but because he does not judge at all, for judgement comes with time, and becomes truth only as time goes on.

The time of the *Critique*, a form of intuition and inner sense, presents the multiplicity of the given only through a constructive activity that is already at work; it gives diversity, but as already contained in the unity of the "I think." In contrast, the time of the Anthropology is assured by a dispersion which cannot be contained, for it is no longer that of the given and passive sensibility; we are dealing with the dispersion of the synthetic activity with regard to itself—dispersion with which it can "Play" as it were. The synthetic activity is not contemporaneous with itself in the organization of multiplicity; it never fails to follow on from itself, thus laying itself open to error, and all the other unsettling slippages (ver*künsteln*, ver*dichten*, ver*rüchen*). While the time of the *Critique* assured the unity of the originary (from the originarily given to the originary synthesis), thus inhering in the dimension of the *Ur...*, that of the *Anthropology* is rooted in the realm of the *Ver...*—and this, because it maintains the dispersion of syntheses as well as the always renewed possibility of seeing them elude one another.[96] Time is not that *in* which, *through* which, and *by* which synthesis is achieved; it wears away the synthetic activity itself. Time affects it, however, not as a given indicating an initial passivity, but as an intrinsic possibility, which raises the hypothesis and the hypothec of an exhaustive determination: the possibility of error is linked to the duty, and to the freedom, to avoid it. That which affects the synthetic activity gives it access to freedom; that which limits it, places it, by that very fact, in an undefined field. In the *Critique*, time made itself transparent to a synthetic activity which was not in itself temporal, because it was constitutive; in the *Anthropology*, time, mercilessly dispersed, serves to obscure, rendering the synthetic acts impenetratable, and swaps the sovereignity of the *Bestimmmung*[97] for the patient, brittle uncertainty under threat from an exercise called *Kunst*.

The word *Kunst* and its derivatives (*verkünsteln, erkünsteln, gekünstelt*) is a term that is often used in the *Anthropology**—and among the most resistant to translation. No art, no technique is meant by it; rather, it refers to the fact according to which nothing is ever given without being at the same time exposed to the dangers of an undertaking which both grounds it in construction and flings it into the arbitrary. The *Kunst* is in one sense the negation of originary passivity, but this negation can and must be understood as spontaneity (with regard to the determinations of diversity) as much as it is artifice (with regard to the solidity of the given); its role is as much to construct an illusion (*Schein*) on top of and facing the phenomenon (*Erscheinung*), as it is to give that illusion the plenitude and the meaning of a phenomenon: which is to say that

---

* See *Anthropology*, pp. 21, 91, 135 and ff.

the *Kunst* restrains—but in the form of freedom—the reciprocal power of negation of the *Schein* and the *Erscheinung*. And even the layers buried deepest within the originary passivity, even that which is most given in the sensible given, are open to this play of freedom: the content of sensible intuition can be used artificially as *Schein*, and that *Schein* can be used intentionally as *Erscheinung*. Thus, in the exchange of the signs of morality, the sensible content can either be nothing more than a mask offering its services to the ruses of deception or, alternatively, the ruse of the ruse, the refined façade which conveys the value and, through the simplicity of an illusion, the importance of the phenomenon.*

The *Kunst* which, at the very foundation of the sensible, already inhabits the whole of the realm of the given, exercises its control in three different ways: as the power of the negative, as the decision of the intentional, as the language of exchange. Thus time, which wears away at the unity of the synthetic act, binding it to a multiplicity, where it will never retrieve its unity in an intemporal sovereignty, opens by this very fact it up to a freedom which is all about exercising negation, giving meaning, establishing communication—a dangerous freedom which relates the work of truth to the possibility of error, and in this way manages to keep the relationship to truth from the sphere of determinations.

The relationship between time and the subject, which was fundamental in the *Critique*, in the *Anthropology* becomes the relationship between time and *Kunst*. In the *Critique*, the subject was aware of itself as "determined in time" and this insurmountable determination referred to the existence of an exterior world with regard to which an internal experience of change was possible;

---

* *Anthropology*, p. 35.

which is to say that time, and the initial passivity that it indicates, was at the root of this *Beziehung auf* that characterizes the first opening of all knowledge. In the *Anthropology*, time and the dispersion that it determines reveal, in the texture of the *Beziehung auf*, a reciprocal belonging to truth and freedom. From the *Critique* to the *Anthropology*—is it not *the same thing* that gets repeated? Time harbours and reveals a "relationship to…," a first opening which is, equally, and at the same time, a bond between truth and freedom—a bond which will, in turn, become the privileged theme of transcendental philosophy and the interrogation which animates the endlessly repeated question of the *Opus Postumum*: *Was ist der Mensch?* And just as the *Beziehung auf* became discernible in the *Critique* through the structure of the *Vorstellung*, so the link between truth and freedom begins to show itself in the *Anthropology* through the work and the perils of *Kunst*.

The *Anthropology* is systematic. Systematic in virtue of a structure which is that of the *Critique*, and which it repeats. But what the *Critique* presents as determination in the relationship between passivity and spontaneity, in the *Anthropology* is described as a temporal dispersion which will never end and has never begun; what concerns anthropology is always already there, and never entirely given; what comes first for anthropology is bound up with a time which in any case envelops it from a distance. It is not that the problem of the origin is unknown to it; on the contrary, it gives the problem back its true meaning, which is not to reveal and to isolate the first time in a single instant, but to recover the temporal framework that, having already begun, is no less radical. The originary is not the *really* primitive, it is the *truly* temporal. That is, it is at the point where, in time, truth and freedom are bonded. There could be a false anthropology—we know all too well what that would look like: it would attempt to go back to a beginning, to an archaism of fact or law, to the structures of the a priori. Kant's *Anthropology* teaches us another lesson: repeat the a priori of the *Critique* in the originary, that is, in a truly temporal dimension.

2) Despite the rootedness of its system, the *Anthropology* is a "popular" work, where "examples can be found by every reader."* What are we to understand by this term? Not a certain kind of content (an empirical analysis cannot but be popular), nor a certain quality of form (a difficult type of knowledge can be 'dressed up' in such a way so as to make it more accessible). A text from the *Logic* lends its status to the notion of *Popularität*.** With regard to knowledge, it is not an addition, an epithet, or a style of expression: it is a kind of *perfection*: … *"eine wahrhaft populäre Vollkommenheit des Erkenntnisses."*[98] It is to be distinguished from technical or scholastic perfection: it is not that they are incompatible, on the contrary,*** it is that the notion of *Popularität* adds something more. In scholastic discourse, we can never be sure whether or not the proof is *"einseitig"*;**** in popular knowledge, on the other hand, there is an exigency which directs it toward the whole, toward exhaustiveness; it does away with the danger of partiality, and thereby authorizes *"einer vollständige Einsicht."****** Its proper

---

* *Anthropology*, Preface, p. 5.

** Logik. Cassirer. T. VIII, pp. 362–363. [In *AA*, vol. IX, pp. 47–48.]

*** Ibid., p. 362. [In *AA*, vol. IX, p. 48.]

**** Ibid., p. 363. [In *AA*, vol. IX, p. 48. *Einseitig*: "one-sided."]

***** Ibid., p. 362. [In *AA*, vol. IX, p. 48. *Einer vollstandige Einsicht*: "a total insight."]

character is thus to be found less in the particularity of a style than in the way in which proof is presented; its arguments are not better (nor worse) than those of scholastic learning—its truth is the same, but with the certainty that the whole is given in the inexhaustible multiplicity of diversity. The various proofs that it offers never give the impression of being biased. Which is just what Kant meant: the reader finds himself in a climate of such total evidence (*vollständige Einsicht*) that he is able to find an unlimited number of new examples.

But "popular knowledge" is not the first, the earliest, nor the most naïve form of truth.

To *become* popular, knowledge has to be based on "*eine Welt und Menschenkenntniss,*"[99] a knowledge of man's concepts, tastes and inclinations.* This sentence from the *Logic* circumscribes the demands of popular knowledge—How can we not consider this the very definition of anthropology?** The *Anthropology*, as a work in the form of "popularity," is grounded in itself in the sense that it is knowledge of man and of the world. "Popular" knowledge and knowledge of the "popular"—in order to exist, it is what it implies.

This circle is not to be undone, but to be taken as it presents itself, where it presents itself—that is, in language. For language offers the possibility of speaking and of speaking about language, and of doing so in the same movement; it is in the everyday use of the inexhaustible source of these "examples" that reading goes on, uninterrupted, and in the familiarity of what is known, writing. To say that a book is popular because readers can find further examples

---

* Ibid., p. 363. [in *AA*, vol. IX, p. 47].

** *Anthropology*, Preface, p. 3.

for themselves is to say that, between the author and the reading public, there is the undivided basis of an everyday language which goes on speaking, without transition and without change, even after the last page. Anthropology, popular knowledge, can find its basis in itself because, speaking a shared language, it speaks of a shared language, and sheds light on it from within. It is therefore a knowledge of man that man himself can immediately understand, recognise, and indefinitely extend—for the two are subject to the same inexhaustible language.

Unlike those texts not intended for a general readership, the *Anthropology* does not set out to define and to justify its vocabulary. On the contrary, it welcomes language in the totality of a use which is never called into question. The *weft* of the text, its empirical guiding thread, is none other than the patient effort to exhaust the verbal forms of a theme, and to give each theme, along with its precise meaning, with its proper scope. The terms used in the eighteenth century in the classification of illnesses, terms such as *einfältig, dumm, Tor, Narr, Geck, unklug,*[100] are accused of being misleading and unnecessary, falling only within a popular use of language, itself based on an obscure and doubtful tradition; they should be replaced by a terminology which supposedly reproduces a logical articulation of the real in the space of nature. Now, it is precisely these words which form the basis and the very substance of Kant's analysis.* It is not a question of ordering the proliferating language of man on the basis of the silent Logos of nature; rather, it is about totalizing this language, on the assumption that every one of its inflections brings with it a particular modality of meaning. The distinction that everyday language makes between *dumm,*

---

* *Anthropology*, p. 96 and ff.

Tor, and *Narr* is just as valid and meaningful as that which, establishing differences in kind, the naturalists make between the terms *vesania* and *insania*. On the anthropological level, there is no such thing as misleading language, nor even an erroneous vocabulary.

In one sense, the Anthropology is a kind of general idiom. Here, well-known expressions are given their full weight. Something is thought in everything that is said. It is enough to ask, and to listen. Why do we often say: *"ein richtiger Verstand, eine geübte Urteilskraft, eine gründliche Vernunft"*?* Is there not something in this which goes straight to the heart of the matter? What serious game is being played out in the opposition between *"eine langweilige Unterredung" and "ein kurzweiliger Mensch"*?** What are we saying when we say *"Geld ist die Lösung?"**** Furthermore, there are all those 'maxims' which, by force of habit, serve as ready-made expressions in the language of man: as guides to etiquette,**** current trends,***** how it is customary to conduct oneself in public.****** They all have their justification. But that justification does not stem from something outside of human practice; nor is it hidden in a distant past: other than a note on the meaning of and the penchant for business amongst the Jews, Kant offers no historical explanations in the *Anthropology.* The meaning of these

---

* Ibid., p. 91. ["Correct understanding, practiced judgment, and thorough reason?"]

** Ibid., p. 129. ["A boring conversation, an entertaining individual." *Langweilig* (boring) literally means "long lasting," whereas *kurzweilig* (entertaining, amusing) is literally "short lasting."]

*** Ibid., p. 174. ["Money is the solution."]

**** Ibid., pp. 18–19.

***** Ibid., p. 142.

****** Ibid., p. 178 and ff.

idiomatic expressions is always of their own time. It is only by pursuing the thread of language and its use, by taking the time to examine both, and by bringing them together in the context of a kind of empirical mapping, that these expressions say what it is that they really want to say. Anthropology is the elucidation of that already established language—whether explicit or silent—through which man engages with things and enters their likenesses into a system of exchange, reciprocity, and silent understanding, which in fact forms neither the republic of minds, nor amounts to the total appropriation of nature but this universal citizenship of man in the world.

The *Anthropology* is thus rooted in a German system of expression and experience. To be sure, Kant tried to extend his analysis beyond this domain by looking at the way foreign languages are spoken, and by referring to other linguistic systems.* No doubt he made use of what was the most particular to his experience so as to overcome its limitations: Königsberg, an administrative capital, university town and business centre, situated at a crossroads and close to the sea, has a guaranteed pedagogical value when it comes to understanding man as a citizen of the whole world.** But all this does not prevent *Anthropology* from inhering situated within geographical and linquistic space from which it cannot quite be dissociated. It is a reflection on and in a system of constituted and all-encompassing signs.

Since the decline of Latin as the universal language of learning and philosophy, the universality of the meaning expressed in modern languages was not, for those who spoke them or heard them, ever in question. For keeping watch over the new language that had

---

* See pp. 120–121 and pp. 128–129, note.

** Ibid., Preface, p. 4, note.

effectively been put to work was the secret law of a Latinity; a law which, although buried, had not yet been absorbed; a law which served to guarantee the intrinsic exchange value of what was said, without remainder. That Kant never fails to assiduously note the equivalent word in Latin throughout the three *Critiques* shows that the universality of his argument is at one with a certain implicit Latinity. The Latin referencing is systematic and essential. In the *Critique of Pure Reason*, Kant is even embarassed by his German, and considers it a limitation. When in his own language he "struggles to find the appropriate expression," he has recourse to "'some dead learned language, even if this means having to restore words to their proper meaning, which having been in use for so long, they had deviated from."* It is better to use Latin than to hamper the "march of science"** by overrefining the German language.

The references to Latin are perhaps as frequent in the *Anthropology* as they are in the *Critiques*. But they are no longer essential, having only the value of signposts and points of reference. Sometimes, they allow Kant to highlight a semantic ambiguity: *Leicht* and *schwer* can mean *light-hearted* and *serious* as well as *easy* and *difficult*.*** At others, they take the place of analysis in the scientific tradition: *Unsinnigkeit-amentia, Wahnsinn-sementia, Wahnwitz-insania, Aberwitz-vesania*.**** At others still, they serve to determine the system of correspondences between critical thought and anthropology. But the real work, the path taken by the thinking in the *Anthropology,* does not pass through this Latinity, rather

---

* Kritik der reinen Vernunft. Cassirer III., p. 275. [*The Critique of Pure Reason*, op. cit., p. 413.]

** Ibid., p. 275, note 1.

*** *Anthropology*, pp. 37–38.

**** Ibid., p. 109.

it is directed by the German system of expression. The term *Melancholia*, for example, does not come close to the true meaning of *Tiefsinnigkeit*; to discover its meaning, one would have to take into account the whole tradition of the German language: the series *Scharfsinnigkeit*,[101] *Leichtsinnigkeit*...[102] etc., on the one hand and, on the other, its subtle opposition, which is not easy to unravel, to the *Tiefdenken*.*[103] Then there is also the lexical field of *Sagen*: *Wahrsagen*, *Vorhersagen*, and *Weissagen*.** And, above all, the great, complex dynasty of *Dichten*.

On the surface, as if on the level of quasi-synonyms, Kant joins words designating other forms of invention, whether psychological or technical, together: *entdecken, entfinden, etwas ausfindig machen, ersinnen, ausdenken, erdichten*.[104] But if we look at the vertical dimension of the text, and follow the thread of the mental powers, we find first the "*Vermögen Ideen zu schaffen*"[105] in a broad sense. Then the ability to give form to those ideas according to the laws of the productive imagination: the *Vermogem zu bilden*. When spiritual power and taste dictate the products of the imagination, we are dealing with *Dichtkunst*[106] in the general sense—which can appeal to the eyes as well as to the ears. Finally, when that art takes the justifiably solemn form of verse, we are dealing with poetry in the strict sense. But, on each of these levels, the *Dichtung*[107] finds itself caught in a an opposition where, if is it not restored to its precise meaning, it risks becoming other than and losing itself: the danger of *Beredsamkeit*,[108] which inverts the relationship between understanding and sensibility; the danger of *Naturmalerei*[109] which limits itself to imitation; the danger

---

* Ibid., p. 107.

** Ibid., p. 80. ["Fortune-telling, predicting, and prophesying."]

of *Versmacherei*,[110] deprived of spiritual power. Thus the complex network of the *Dichtung* is identified and defined thanks to the totalization of the lexical field to which it belongs.* Yet the faculties thus revealed do not, in their structure, serve as the guiding thread of the analysis; rather, the powers are glimpsed through the web of words such it is knotted together through so many years of daily use. To be sure, Kant occasionally corrects how people speak, picking up on such and such ambiguity;** but he does so in the name of a distinction which really exists, so as to denounce those who, speaking hurriedly, do not make use of it, considering it null and void.

That philosophical reflection broke away from the universality of the Latin form in this way is important. Henceforth, philosophical language would see that it was possible to locate its place of origin, and to define its field of exploration, within a given linguistic system. That this language be linked to a linguistic system does not serve to relativize or to limit the meaning that it bears, but locates the discovery of that meaning within a determined lexical field. This connection between philosophical meaning and the meanings given in a linguistic system—which will turn out to be so decisive for German thought—is not yet reflected upon in and of itself in the *Anthropology*, even if it is appealed to at every instant: the real grounds of the anthropological experience is far more linguistic than it is psychological. And yet, language is not yet presented as a system to be interrogated, but rather as an element which goes without saying, in which we find ourselves from the beginning; an instrument of exchange, a vehicule for dialogue, a

---

* Ibid., p. 143 and ff.

** Ibid., p. 80.

form of virtual understanding, language is what philosophy and nonphilosophy have in common. It is in language that the one meets the other—or rather, that they communicate.

There is, then, a Kantian *Banquet*—the insistence in the *Anthropology* on communal meals, those miniscule units of society; the importance of the *Unterhaltung*,[111] of what is and what must be exchanged there; the prestige of the moral and social model of a *Gesellschaft*[112] where everyone is connected and, at the same time, everyone is sovereign; the value of the discourse which, in the dialogue between one person to another, and engaging everyone, emerges and is realized. From the point of view of anthropology, the grouping which has a paradigmatic value is not the family, nor the state, but the *Tischgesellschaft*.[113] For, when it faithfully obeys its own rules, the *Tischgesellschaft* looks like the particular image of universality.* There, through the transparency of a common language, a bond linking everyone has to be established: no one should feel privileged, and no one should feel isolated; everybody, whether speaking or silent, has to be present together in the shared sovereignty of speech. None of the three major functions of language should be left out: statement of contingent fact (*Erzählen*); formulation, exchange, and rectification of judgement (*Räsonieren*); free-play of language with itself (*Scherzen*). It is essential that each of these three functions takes turn to hold sway in a movement that is the proper rhythm of this kind of gathering: first, the novelty of the event, then the gravity of the universal, and finally the irony of play. As for the content of the conversation itself, it must obey the laws of an internal structure: those of a flexible continuity, which procedes without break, so

* The rules of a "geschmackvollen Gastmahls" ["tasteful banquet"] are set out on p. 179 and ff.

that each person's freedom to formulate his or her opinion, to insist upon it or to take the conversation in another direction, is never felt by others to be an abuse or a constraint. Thus, in the regulated aspect of language, the expression of freedoms and the possibility, for individuals, of gathering together to form a whole, can happen spontaneously, without the intervention from an outside force or authority, renunciation, or alienation. By speaking within the community of a Convivium, freedoms encounter one another and, spontaneously, are universalized. Everyone is free, but in the form of totality.

We should no longer be surprised by the promise made at the beginning of the *Anthropology*, which was to study man as a 'citizen of the world'—a promise which the book seemed to go back on, by limiting itself to an analysis of the *Gemüt*.* In fact, anthrolopogy's man is indeed a *Weltbürger*, but not in the sense that he belongs to a given social group or such and such institution. He is *Weltbürger* purely and simply because he speaks. It is in the exchange of language that he manages on his own account both to attain and to realize the concrete universal. His living in the world is, originarily, residence in language.

The truth that anthropology brings to light is therefore not a truth anterior to language, and that that language will be entrusted to convey. It is a truth that is both more interior and more complex: it is in the very movement of the exchange, and that exchange realizes the universal truth of man. Just as, earlier, we saw how the originary could be defined as temporality itself, we can now say that the originary is not to be found in an already given, secret meaning, but in what is the most manifest path of the

---

* See above, p. 56.

exchange. It is here that language takes, realizes, and rediscovers its reality; it is also here that man exhibits his anthropological truth.

The *Anthropology* is therefore "systematically projected" by a reference to the *Critique* which works across time; it also has the value of popularity because its thinking is situated within a given language that it makes transparent without reformulating it, for the very particularities of that language are the legitimate birthplace of universal significations. From an anthropological perspective, then, truth takes its shape through the temporal dispersion of syntheses and in the movement of language and exchange; there, it does not find its most primitive form, nor the moments leading to its constitution, nor indeed the pure shock of the already given; it finds, in a time that has already elapsed, and in a language which is already spoken, within a temporal flux and a linguistic system never given at degree zero, something like its original form: the universal emerges from the very heart of experience in the movement of the *truly temporal* and the *actually exchanged*. It is in this way that the analysis of the *Gemüt* (in the form of inner sense) becomes cosmopolitan prescription (in the form of human universality).

We saw above how, through the very repetition of the *Critique*, anthropological thinking constitutes the moment of the passage into transcendental philosophy. It is easy to see how this repetition might acquire the structure, function, and value of a transition: even if the repetition of the *Critique* occurs on a straightforwardly empirical level, it is repeated on this level in such a way that the syntheses of truth (which is to say, the constitution of the necessary in the realm of experience) henceforth appear in the domain of freedom (in the recognition of the particular as universal subject).

The *Anthropology* repeats the *Critique of Pure Reason* on an empirical level where the *Critique of Practical Reason* finds itself already repeated: the realm of the necessary is also the domain of the imperative.* The *Anthropology* is therefore essentially the investigation of a field where the practical and the theoretical intersect with and cover one another entirely; it repeats, in the same place and in the same language, the a priori of knowledge and the moral imperative—and, in doing so, through the movement of this empirical discourse which is its very own, it initiates what it postulates: a transcendental philosophy where the correlation between truth and freedom is defined from the very beginning. In other words, this anthropologico-critical repetition is grounded neither in itself nor in the *Critique*: it is based on a fundamental thinking, with regard to which the *Anthropology*—which has neither the substance of the repeated, nor the depth of that which grounds the repetition, and which therefore amounts only to the transitional but necessary moment of repetition—cannot but erase itself, and disappear, paradoxically, as having been essential.

Initiated by *Anthropology* but also, by the very fact of that overture, soon free of it, transcendental philosophy is thus able to deal, on its own level, with the problem that, at *Anthropology*'s insistence, it was forced it to unveil: the bond between truth and freedom. For it is this very relationship that is in question in the

---

* Which is what is no doubt foreseen in *The Critique of Practical Reason* where, in the empirical domain, anthropology is the counterpoint to physical science, but where it is also governed by Ethics. It is therefore not a question of a pragmatic anthropology and no allusion is made to a "physiological" anthropology which would belong to the domain of nature. (Vorrede. Cassirer, t. IV, p. 7) [*The Critique of Practical Reason*, in I. Kant, *Practical Philosophy*, op. cit., p. 142.]

great tripartition that is repeated constantly throughout the *Opus Postumum*: God, the world, and man. God who is "*Persönlichkeit*," who is freedom, who is, with regard to man and to the world, absolute *source*; world that is the whole, closed in on itself, of the objects of experience, that is truth, and impassable *domain*; as for man, he is their synthesis—that which in God and the world actually unify. And yet, with regard to the world he is only one of its inhabitants, and with regard to God only a *limited* being. Which is enough of an indication that the bond between truth and freedom takes the form of finitude, and in this way brings us back to the very root of critical thought. We are at the level of that which grounds the refusal of an intuitive intellect.

These three terms, God, the world, and man, in their fundamental relationship to one another, get these notions of *source, domain,* and *limit* going again—the organizational persistence and force of which we have already seen at work in Kantian thought. It was these three notions which obscurely governed over the three essential questions of the *Philosophieren* and the *Critiques*; it was the same three notions which made explicit the content of the *Anthropology*; now, they lend their transcendental meaning to the questions raised by God taken as an ontological source, the world as the domain of existences, and by man as the synthesis of the two in the form of finitude. And perhaps it is precisely because the reign of these questions appears so universal and so polymorphous, so transgressive with regard to all possible division, that they lead to an understanding of the link between critical thinking and an *Anthropology* and between an *Anthropology* and a transcendental philosophy. The *Critique*, interrogating the links between passivity and spontaneity—that is, the a priori—asks a sequence of questions on the basis of the notion of *Quellen*.[114] The *Anthropology*, interrogating the links between temporal dispersion and the universality of language—that is, the *originary*—is situated within the problematic which is that of a world already given, of an *Umfang*.[115] Transcendental philosophy, seeking to define the relationship between truth and freedom—that is, situating itself in the realm of the *fundamental*—cannot fail to come up against the problem of finitude, of *Grenzen*.[116]

Doubtless it is in the recurrence of these three notions, their fundamental rootedness, that the movement according to which the conceptual destiny, that is, the problematic, of contemporary philosophy can be seen to take shape: that dispersion which no confusion, dialectical or phenomenological, will have the right to reduce, and which divides up the field of all philosophical reflection according to the *a priori*, the *originary*, and the *fundamental*. Since Kant, the implicit project of all philosophy has been to overcome this essential division, to the point where it becomes clear that such overcoming cannot take place outside of a thinking which repeats it, and by repeating it, instates it. *Anthropology* is precisely the site where that confusion will be reproduced, incessantly. Whether it is referred to as such, or concealed in other projects, *Anthropology*, or at least the anthropological level of reflection, will come to alienate philosophy. The intermediary character of the originary and, with it, of anthropological analysis, situated between the a priori and the fundamental, is what allows it to function as an impure and unthought hybrid within the internal economy of philosophy: it will be accorded both the privileges of the a priori and the meaning of the fundamental, the preliminary character of critical thought and the realized form of transcendental philosophy; it makes no distinction between the problematic of the necessary and that of existence; it confuses the analysis of conditions with the interrogation of finitude. One day, the whole history of post-Kantian and contemporary philosophy will have to be envisaged from the point of view of the perpetuation of this confusion—a revised history which would start out by denouncing it.

Doubtless, this "destructuring" of the philosophical field, has never been more sensitively undertaken than in the wake of phenomenology. To be sure, it was Husserl's initial project—such as it is set out in the *Logische Untersuchungen*[117]—to liberate those regions of the a priori of forms that reflection on the *originary* had been deprived of. But, because the originary can never itself serve as the grounds for its own liberation, in the end the task of getting away from the originary conceived as immediate subjectivity falls to the originary conceived in the density of passive syntheses and the already there. The reduction gives rise to a transcendental illusion, and never manages to play the role destined for it—which was to reserve a place for an elided critical reflection. Even the reference to Descartes,[118] which, at one point in Husserl's thinking, takes over from the predominance of Kantian remembrances, does not succeed in masking this structural imbalance. As soon as all openings onto the realm of the fundamental stop short of directing us toward what should have been its justification and its meaning, the problematic of the *Welt* and the *In-der-Welt* is open to the hypothec of empiricity. All forms of phenomenological psychology, and all the other variations on the analysis of existence, bear doleful testimony to this.

What form of blindness prevents us from seeing that the authentic articulation of the *Philosophieren* was once again present, and in a far more restrictive form, in a thinking that was perhaps not itself aware of what it owed in terms of filiation and fidelity to the old "Chinaman of Königsberg"?[119] We would probably have to know what "to philosophize with a hammer"[120] means, take a preliminary look at what the *Morgenrot*[121] is, to understand what comes back to us in the Eternal return to see there the authentic repetition, in a world that is our own, of what was, for an already distant culture, reflection on the a priori, the originary and finitude. For it is there, in that thinking which thought the end of philosophy, that the possibility of continuing to philosophize, and the injunction of a new austerity, resides.

A problem remains—one that the movement of Kantian thought does very little to help unravel: that of empiricity in the anthropologico-critical repetition. Must we consider this tendency toward empiricity an essential aspect of any thinking that wants to find a path from the a priori to the fundamental? If so, then a science of man—or, rather, the empirical field in which the science of man is possible—naturally fits into philosophy's trajectory toward itself. Or can we conceive of an anthropology which does not find its content and its laws in empiricity, but which deals with essences in a mode of reflecting on man that only intuition can enrich and enliven? There, the empirical would only have the value of an example, and would neither define nor compromise the form of the knowledge itself.

Kant's *Anthropology* offers no clear response to this. To be sure, it amounts to nothing more than a collection of empirical examples; but, precisely because it is nothing more than a collection and rhapsody of examples, the reflexive movement which divides it comes from elsewhere and is directed elsewhere, without the *mode of support* offered by the empirical ground this knowledge covers ever being clearly defined. There is a double system of solidarity at work in the *Anthropology*: solidarity with critical reflection and transcendental philosophy on the one hand and, on the other, with a whole series of anthropological researches which were being undertaken, primarily in Germany, in the second half of the eighteenth century.

Working out how Kant's book fits into the chronology and the network of influence amongst these anthropological texts is by no means straightforward. For two reasons: the first is that Kantian thought already had a hold over the science and, in particular, over the psychology and medicine of the time; the other is the delay in publishing the *Anthropology*, a delay which enabled the dissemination of his students' notes and textbooks—such as those that Starke would use some forty years later.[122] While it is the case that many texts published prior to the *Anthropology* refer explicitly or implicitly to Kantian thought, the dates of publication are unreliable, making it impossible to establish the chain of influence and order of precedence. To help us to navigate out way through this complex network, we have only three kinds of landmarks:

1) Those texts which make an explicit reference to Kant, as in Ith's *Versuch einer Anthropologie* (Bern 1794), Schmid's *Empirische Psychologie* (Iena 1791), and Hufeland's *Makrobiotik*. We have already indicated the references that these texts make to Kant. But we should also add the second edition of Platner's *Anthropology** to this list, as well as other works which are written directly under

---

* Platner makes reference to Kant in t. 1., p. 52. [Ernst Platner (1744–1818) was at first a Professor of Medicine and then a Professor of Philosophy in Leipzig. He wrote an *Anthropologie für Aerzte und Weltweise*, published in Leipzig in 1772 and reprinted as *Neue Antropologie für Aerzte und Weltweise, mit besonderer Rücksicht auf Physiologie, Pathologie, Moralphilosophie und Aesthetik. 1. Band*, Leipzig: S. L. Crusius, 1790.]

Kant's influence, such as Köllner's "Bestimmung der organischen Kräfte nach Grundsätzen der kritischen Philosophie."*

2) On the other hand, the fact that certain texts were published earlier authorizes us to presume that Kant was aware of them and made use of them in his *Anthropology*. At the top of this list we should probably put Tetens' *Versuch über die menschliche Natur* (1777),[123] Platner's *Anthropology* (1772), and of course Baumgarten's *Psychologia Empirica* (1749).[124] This work, which Kant annotated,** serves as the *Anthropology*'s guiding thread. The correspondence between the two texts in terms of organization is striking—you could superimpose them paragraph by paragraph.*** Once again we should note that both follow the classic prescription of eighteenth century psychology, which no doubt originated in Wolff.**** But there is more to it than that. Baum-

---

* In *Archiv für die Physiologie*, 1797. T. II, p. 240 and ff. [See J. Köllner, *Prüfung der neuesten Bemühungen und Untersuchungen in der Bestimmung der organischen Kräfte nach Grundsätzen der kritischen Philosophie*, von D. Joh. Christ. Reil (editor), Halle, In der Curtschen Buchhandlung, 1795–1815, vol. 2, 1797, pp. 240–350.]

** The notes can be found in T. XV of *Kants Schriften* published by the Academy [in *AA*. See above p. 20 fn., p. 21 fn., and below p. 142, fn.6.]

*** The Table of Contents of Baumgarten's book is as follows: I. Existentia animae; II. Facultas cognitiva inferior; III. Sensus (internus, externi); IV. Phantasia; V. Perspicacia; VI. Memoria; VII. Facultas fingerdi; VIII. Praevisio; IX. Judicium; X. Praesagitio; XI. Facultas characteristica. XII. Intellectus; XIII. Ratio; XIV. Indifferentia; XV. Voluptas et taedium; XVI. Facultas appetitiva. [See Baumgarten, *Metaphysik*, op. cit., §§ 504–675].

**** See Wolff, Logica (Francfurt 1728) [See Christian Wolff (1679–1754), *Philosophia rationalis, sive Logica, methodo scientifica pertractata et ad usum scientiarum atque vitae aptata*, (Frankfurt and Leipzig, 1728) in *Gesammelte Schriften*, II. Abt., vol. 1., Pars I–III, edited by Jean École. Georg Olms, Hildesheim, Zürich, New York, 1983.]

garten's *Psychology* furnished Kant with schemas that are taken up and elaborated upon in the *Anthropology*: the distinction between *"perceptio primaria"* and *"perceptio adhaerens"** becomes in the *Anthropology* the doubled-up system of *perceptio primaria et secundaria* and of *"perceptio principalis et adhaerens."*** The same goes for Baumgarten's analysis of *Wahrsagen* and *Weissagen,**** which in Kant's book is spelt out in a distinction made between *Vorhersagen, Wahrsagen,* and *Weissagen.*****

3) Finally—and without fear of commiting any serious error—we can identify the influence of certain texts on the development of Kant's work. Some of the changes made and new passages added to the final draft of the *Anthropology* stem from recently published texts. We can be sure, for example, that Kant had read Schmid's *Empirische Psychologie*, and that he made use of it. In Nachlass's[125] notes in the lectures published by Starke, there is no mention whatsoever of the empirical sources that aided and supported anthropological thinking. It is only in the 1798 text that we see any mention made of the *Hilfsmittel*[126] which, in the order they appear, are: the history of the world, biographies, theatre and novels.***** Now, in 1791, Schmid devoted a paragraph of the *Hilfsmittel* to the empirical study of the soul: history books, biographies, notes on character, tragic and cosmic poetry, the novel.****** More significantly still, the same Schmid distinguishes between three sorts of

---

* § 530. *Kants Schriften*. Ak. XV. p. 11 [in *AA*].

** *Anthropology*, pp. 26–27.

*** § 516. *Kants Schriften*. Ak. XV. p. 31 [in *AA*].

**** *Anthropology*, p. 80 [§ 36: "Predicting, fortune-telling, prophesying."]

***** Ibid., Preface, p. 5.

****** Schmid, *Empirische Psychologie*. Vorrede in fine [op. cit., see p. 21 fn.]

human sciences: everything to do with man's interior world (*sein Inneres*) and inner sense is called *psychology*; everything to do with exteriority (*sein Äusseres*) and with the body is called *medical anthropology*; as for *anthropology properly speaking*, it has to do with the study of the interrelations between the interior and the exterior.* It is hard not to think that this was where the subtitles that, from 1791 on, Kant would give to the two sections of the *Anthropology*, came from.**

There was, then, a whole network of empirical knowledge which, at the end of the eighteenth century constituted the field of anthropology. The affinity between this ensemble and Kant's text is clear, even if it is still not possible to identify precisely the chronological order of the connections or the hierarchy of reciprocal influences. But we can now investigate the more general meaning of this field of empirical knowledge which, at the time, had just emerged and which sought to found a new science: anthropology.

Let us put the archaeology of a term—whose form, if not its fate, was determined in the sixteenth century—to one side.*** What meaning do these new anthropologies have in relation to the Cartesian version of the science of man?

---

* Ibid., p. 11.

** See supra p. 70.

*** See for example Cregut: *Dissertatio de Anthropologia* (1737) where anthropology is defined as: "Sermo de homine." (p. 2) [The author's name is difficult to read, but appears to be: Friedrich Christian Cregut (1675–1758), *Dissertatio de anthropologia*, in Johann Gottfried von Berger (1659–1736), *Physiologia medica: sive De natura humana liber bipartitvs. Iterum in lucem prodit cura Frider. Christiani Cregut ... cujus Dissertatio De anthropologia ejusque præcipuis tam antiquis quam modernis scriptoribus introductionis loco praemittitur*, Francofurti: Stock & Schilling, 1737.]

1) It would appear that, at the beginning of the eighteenth century, the initial project of anthropology related to an ensemble of precise scientific problems: what we too readily refer to as the critique of the Cartesian mechanism was, at the time, merely a means to articulate, in a theoretical idiom, the new kind of intellectual labour they were engaged in. Generally speaking, research into the functioning of the human body at the time prompted a major conceptual split: in the unity of the *physis*, which is not in question, what is *physical* for *a body* begins to be distinguished from that which, for *bodies* in the plural, is of the order of the *physics*. What is physical in man is of nature, but nevertheless not of physics. Hence the curious, and sometimes contradictory, conceptual cross-fertilization of ideas, all of which come back to this difficulty in organizing the relationship between the knowledge of physics, of the physical, and of physis. Wolff holds onto the "physica" as the most general kind of knowledge of nature, and, within that, names the science of the body "physiology."* In contrast, Kant groups all empirical knowledge of nature under the heading "physiology," of which "physics" only covers a small area.** Indeed, if nowadays natural science seems to be at odds with physics, it is because, since Kant, physics can no longer cover the domain of the human body. The existence of anthropology is at once the cause and the effect, or in any case the measure of this variance between the two.

2) But why should this variance be linked to an anthropology and not to a general biology? Why does Wolff say that physiology is a science "*de corpore animati, praesertim humano*"?*** Doubtless

---

* Wolff. *Logica*. § 84. (Frankfurt. 1728) p. 37. [in *Gesammelte Schriften*, op. cit.]

** See above, p. 56.

*** Wolff. Ibid. [*Philosophia Rationalis sive Logica* in *Gesammelte Schriften*, op. cit., § 84, p. 37: "concerning the living body, notably the human."]

because knowledge of man is to be found at the juncture between the determination of a metaphysical privilege that is the soul and the mastery of technique that is medicine. Man is therefore the first theme of knowledge that could have emerged in the field left empty by the variance between physis and physics. "*Definitur Physiologia per scientiam corporis animati; strictius a medius per scientiam corporis sani; alii tractationem physicam de homine in specie Anthropologiam vocant.*"*

It is in the sense that physiology is anthropology that it acquires its specificity; anthropology is its reason for not being physics pure and simple.

3) The paradoxical stance adopted by *Anthropology* (it is the *reason* for what it is a *part* of) is laden with consequences. It means that anthropology is both the limit of the science of physis and is the science of that limit; it is the limit worn away, falling short of itself, of the domain that it delimits, and so defines the nonrelation in terms of relation, rupture in terms of continuity, finitude in terms of positivity. Platner said: "consideration of the body and soul in their reciprocal relations, limitations and connections—that is what I would call anthropology."** But Telena[127] had quite rightly seen that, in anthropology, that relationship could only ever be circumscribed from the point of view of physis. And that this would be in opposition to their philosophical method; according to Telena, changes in the soul should be taken "*wie sie durch das Selbstgefühl erkannt werden*";[128] in analytical psychology, or anthropology, he

---

* Wolff. Ibid. ["Physiology is defined as the science of the living body; more specifically, as a means to a science of the healthy body; others consider the physical treatise on man to be a kind of anthropology."]

** Platner. *Anthropologie*, p. 17. [op. cit. See above p. 109.]

considers the changes in the soul *"von der Seit da sie etwas in dem Gehirn als dem inner Organ der Seele sind,"*[129] and are to be explained *"als solche Gehirnsbeschaffenheiten und Veränderungen."*[*][130]

4) Because of what was most initiatory in its project, anthropology cannot help being both reductive and normative. Reductive, because it refuses to accept what man already knows of himself, by the *"Selbstgefühl,"*[131] but also what he might find out in the process that involves the mediation of physis. Anthropology concerns only the phenomenon of the phenomemon, at the conclusion of a flexion which always implies the horizon of Nature. On the other hand, it will always be the science of a living body, finalized with regard to itself, developing on the basis of a sound functioning. Anthropology is the knowledge of a well-being which, for man, is synonymous with life. It is, in some ways, the science of the normal par excellence: *"Die Lehre von der Beschaffenheit von dem Nutzen der Teile des menschlichen Körpers im gesunden Zustand."*[**]

5) In this way, anthropology both encircles and envelops all knowledge of man. It serves as the explicit or implicit horizon of everything that man can know of himself. And, in the sense that they all have something to do with man, every other area of scientific

---

* Tetens: *Philosophische Versuche über die menschliche Natur.* (Vorrede. p. IV). [Johann Nicolas Tetens (1736–1807, a mathematician, physician and philosopher), *Philosophische Versuche über die menschliche Natur und ihre Entwicklung,* Leipzig: M. G. Weidmanns Erben und Reich, 1777: "He considers the modifications of the soul as 'existing within the brain as the inner organ of the soul' and seeks to explain them 'as constituting and indicating changes within the brain.'"]

** Loder, *Anfangsgründe der Medicinale Antropologie* (1793). [Just Christian Loder, *Anfangsgründe der physiologischen Anthropologie und der Stats-Arzneykunde...,* 3rd edition, Weimar: im Verlage des Industrie-Comptoirs, 1800: "The doctrine of the human body in a healthy state."]

inquiry is placed within the vast field of anthropology: "The first object that strikes me in this vast ensemble of our knowledge is that which deals with man considered in his personal relationships, and men gathered together in political groupings."* But as a natural being, man grounds his knowledge only by limiting it, only by engaging in the play of nature which offers him the possibility of knowledge by withdrawing its value. So an anthropologically-based science is a science reduced, science on a man-made scale, devoid of its own truth, but which, for that very reason, restored to the truth of man. It is in this way that anthropology, being at once a foundation and a reductive rule, begins to look like a form of normative knowledge, one that preemptively prescribes its teaching, its possibilities, and its limitations to every other form of scientific inquiry that engages with man. Hence Ith's premonition of different kinds of anthropology: one would be physiological, another psychological, a third historical, and a fourth moral or teleological.** Serving as the basis for knowledge, or at least constituting the science which serves as the basis for knowledge, anthropology limits and finalizes it in a single movement.

Whatever its empirical content, then, anthropology has an epistemological structure of its very own. That structure has a meaning which cannot be superimposed onto the "Treatises on

---

* Lacretelle: *De l'établissement des connaissances humaines* (1792, p. 52). [Pierre-Louis Lacretelle (1751–1824), *De l'établissement des connoissances humaines et de l'instruction publique dans la Constitution française*, Paris: Chez Desenne, 1791.]

** *Versuch einer Anthropologie*, Bern 1795. I, pp. 78–79. [op. cit., see above, p. 22.] See also Voss: *Grundriss einer vorbereitender Anthropologie* (Halle. 1791). [Christian Daniel Voß (Professor at Halle), *Grundriss einer vorbereitenden Antropologie zunächst für gelehrte Schulen und Gymnasien entworfen.*]

Man"—which, at least in style, is still in the Cartesian tradition—nor onto the empiricisms which have always dominated Locke's thinking.[132] Evidently, like the former, it is a knowledge articulated in the language of nature and, like the latter, it designates the originary. But these are just instances in the context of its total epistemological structure. That structure in fact pivots on something that is neither animal nor human: not self-consciousness, but *Menschenwesen*. Which is to say: that which is at once man's natural being, the law of his possibilities, and the a priori limit of his knowledge. Anthropology is therefore not only the science of man, as well as being the science and the horizon of all human sciences, but also the science of that which founds and limits man's knowledge for him. Herein lies the ambiguity of this *Menschen-Kenntniss* which characterises anthropology: it is the knowledge of man, in a movement which objectifies man on the level of his natural being and in the content of his animal determinations; at the same time, it is the knowledge of the knowledge of man, and so can interrogate the subject himself, ask him where his limitations lie, and about what he sanctions of the knowledge we have of him.

Anthropology believed that it was calling a sector of nature into question; in fact, it was asking a question which would cast, over the philosophy of our time, the shadow of a classical philosophy henceforth deprived of God: *Is it possible to have empirical knowledge of finitude?* Although Cartesian thinking had confronted this finitude very early on, as early as the experience of error, it was only by undertaking an ontology of the infinite that it could be definitively dismissed. As for empiricism, it practiced this finitude, referring to it incessantly, but as much as its own limitation as the frontier of knowledge. The anthropological interrogation of finitude is of a different order: for anthropology, it is question of knowing if, on the level of man, a knowledge of finitude can exist, a knowledge sufficiently liberated and grounded so as to be able think that finititude in itself—that is, as a form of positivity.

It is here that the major reorganization undertaken by Kant intervenes. The internal structure of *Anthropology* and the question which secretly animates the book in fact take the same form as critical enquiry itself: it, too, presumes to know the possibilities and the limitations of knowledge; from a position of exteriority, it mimicks, in the gestures of empiricity, the movement of critical philosophy; furthermore, what it takes as *given* seems to be able to function as an a priori. For a long time, the "anthropologists" thought that they could absorb Kant's teachings without any difficulty, without any rethinking on their part being required: Schmid, Hufeland, and Ith are the first to attest to this, but the list could go on and on, and is by no means confined to the eighteenth century. It would take the inflexible naivety of our contemporaries to congratulate anthropology for having at last moved beyond the dissociations—between body and soul, subject and object—in which the drought of rationalism would otherwise have been lost. But what they took to be the marvel of renconcilation was in fact just the more predicatable miracle of their failure to register the grammatical ambiguity of *Menschenkenntniss*.

In fact, the moment we think that we can give critical thought the value of positive knowledge, we will have forgotten the essential point of Kant's lesson. The difficulty we encountered in situating the *Anthropology* in relation to the critical ensemble ought to have been indication enough that the lesson is not simple. What Kant teaches us is that *Anthropology*'s empiricity cannot be grounded in itself, that it is possible only on account of the repetition of the *Critique*, that it therefore cannot contain the *Critique*; but that could not help referring to it; and if the *Anthropology* looks like the extrinsic and empirical *analogon* of the *Critique* it is because it is based on the structures of the a priori that had already been identified and made known. In the general organization of Kantian thought, finitude can therefore never be thought on its own level; it presents itself to knowledge and to discourse only in a secondary fashion; but that to which it is bound to refer is not an ontology of the infinite; rather, it is, in their organization of the ensemble, the a priori conditions of knowledge. Which is to say that *Anthropology* finds itself doubly beholden to critical thought: as knowledge, it relies on the conditions that it sets and the realm of experience that it determines; as an investigation of finitude, it relies on the first, impassable forms that critical thought makes manifest.

Thus understood, the job of *Anthropology* bears some resemblance to that of the *Anfangsgründe der Natur*.[133] to reveal the system of articulation between critical thought and the a priori forms of knowledge on the one hand, and, on the other, to reveal, in the *Critique*, the principles of an empirically constituted and historically developed knowledge. But lying beneath this apparent symmetry is a profound dissymmetry: in the *Anfangsgründe*, it is a question of physics, and thus of a science constituted in its plenitude and its truth; in the *Anthropology*, we are dealing with physis, and so with that layer of knowledge which deals with imperfections, frontiers, and failings—in short, with negativity in nature. In other words, the continuity from the *Critique* to the *Anfangsgründe* is guaranteed by the forms of symmetrical activity and the truth that critical thought establishes and structures; between the *Critique* and the *Anthropology*, the continuity is given by the fact that both insist on limitations, and on the inflexibility of the finitude that they gesture toward. The *Foundations of Natural Science* does without God and renders the hypothesis of an actual infinity—the internal contradiction of which critical thought made clear—futile; the *Anthropology* indicates the absence of God, and occupies the void that the infinite leaves in its wake. No doubt the reciprocal inversion, the dissymmetrical symmetry of the *synthesis* and the *limit*, are at the heart of Kantian thought: this is the source from which the *Critique* draws its privileges with regard to all possible knowledge.

It is now time to return to the problem we began with—how the critical enterprise was accompanied by the lectures on anthropology, that unchanging counterpoint in relation to which Kant redoubled the effort of transcendental reflection through the constant accumulation of empirical knowledge of man. That Kant taught anthropology for twenty-five years stems from something more than the demands of university life; this persistence is linked to the very structure of the Kantian problem: How to think, analyse, justify, and ground finitude in a thinking which does not take the path of an ontology of the infinite and does not find its justification in a philosophy of the absolute? The question is effectively at work in the Anthropology but, because it cannot be thought for itself in the context of an empirical enquiry, it cannot assume its true dimensions there. Hence the *marginal* character of anthropology with regard to the Kantian enterprise: it is at once essential and inessential—a border that is peripheral to the centre, but which never stops referring to and interrogating it. One could say that the critical movement *broke away from* the anthropological structure, both because the latter gives it its outline, and because the critical movement acquires its value only by breaking free of anthropology, by turning against it, and, in so doing, by grounding it. The epistemological configuration proper to anthropology mimicks that of the *Critique*; but it was a question of how to avoid getting caught up in the prestige that this affords, and how to reinstate the rational order of this resemblance. That order used to consist in making the *Anthropology* gravitate around the *Critique*. And that order reinstated was, for anthropology, the authentic form of its liberation—the revelation of its true meaning: the Anthropology could now emerge as that in which the transition from the a priori to the fundamental, from critical thought to transcendental philosophy, is announced.

We see what web of confusion and illusion anthropology and contemporary philosophy are tangled up in. One aim has been to make the Anthropology count as a Critique, as a critique liberated from the prejudices and the dead weight of the a priori, overlooking the fact that it can give access to the realm of the fundamental only if remains under the sway of critical thought. Another (which is just another version of the same oversight) has been to turn anthropology into a positive field which would serve as the basis for and the possibility of all the human sciences, whereas in fact it can only speak the language of the limit and of negativity: its sole purpose is to convey, from the vigour of critical thought to the transcendental foundation, the precedence of finitude.

In the name of what is—that is to say what ought to be on the basis of its essence—anthropology within the field of philosophy as a whole, we challenge all those "philosophical anthropologies" that present themselves as the natural access to the fundamental, as well as all those philosophies which define their starting point and their scope through a certain kind of anthropological reflection on man. In both, we find the play of an "illusion" proper to Western philosophy since Kant. In its anthropological form, it serves as the counterpoint to the transcendental illusion harboured by pre-Kantian metaphysics. It will be by way of symmetry and taking the latter as our guiding thread that we will come to an understanding of what the anthropological illusion consists in.

For the one effectively derives historically from the other—or, rather, it is thanks to a shift in the meaning given to the transcendental illusion in Kantian critique that the anthropological illusion could emerge. The necessary character of the emergence of the transcendental is frequently interpreted, not as a structure of truth, phenomenon and experience, but as one of the concrete marks of finitude. But what Kant had ambiguously designated as "natural" in that emergence had been forgotten as a fundamental form of the relationship to the object and resurrected as the "nature" in human nature. As a result, instead of being defined by the movement that criticized it in the context of a reflection on knowledge, the illusion was submitted to an anterior level where it reemerged as both divided and grounded: it had become the truth of truth—henceforth, truth would be always present and yet never given; thus the illusion had become both the raison d'etre and the source of critical thinking, the origin of that movement by which man loses sight of and is incessantly recalled to truth. The illusion henceforth defined as finitude would become above all else the *retreat* of truth: that in which truth hides and in which truth can always be found.

It is in this way that, from a structural point of view, the anthropological illusion looks like the reverse, the mirror image of the transcendental illusion. The latter consisted in the application of the principles of understanding beyond the limits of experience, and thus in admitting an actual infinite to the field of possible knowledge through a kind of spontaneous transgression. The anthropological illusion resides in a reflexive regression which has to answer for that transgression. Finitude is only gone beyond if it is something other than itself, if it rests on a shortfall in which it finds its source; it falls short, it is itself, but withdrawn from the field of experience where it is encountered and introduced into the realm of the originary in which it is grounded. The problem of finitude goes from interrogating the limit and transgression[134] to interrogating the return to the self; from a problematic of truth to a problematic of the same and other. It has entered into the domain of alienation.

And the paradox is this: freeing itself from a preliminary critique of knowledge and an initial interrogation of the relationship to the object, philosophy did not manage to free itself from subjectivity as the fundamental thesis and starting point of its enquiry. On the contrary, it locked itself into subjectivity by conceiving of it as thickened, essentialized, enclosed in the impassable structure of *"menschliches Wesen,"* in which that extenuated truth which is the truth of truth keeps vigil and gathers itself.

We can now see why, in a single movement, characteristic of the thinking of our time, all knowledge of man is presented as either dialecticized from the start or fully dialecticizable—as always invested with a meaning which has to do with the return to the origin, to the authentic, to the founding activity, to the reason why there is meaning in the world. We can also see why all philosophy presents itself as capable of communicating directly with the sciences of man or empirical studies of man without having to take a detour through a critique, an epistemology, or a theory of knowledge. Anthropology is the secret path which, orientated toward the foundations of our knowledge, connects, in the form of an unthought mediation, man's experience with philosophy. The values implicit in the question *Was its der Mensch?* are responsible for this homogenous, de-structured and infinitely reversible field in which man presents his truth as the soul of truth. The polymorphous notions of "meaning," "structure," and "genesis"—whatever value they might have, and which a rigorous reflection ought to restore to them—here indicate only the confusion of the domain in which they assume their communicative roles. That these notions circulate indiscriminately throughout the human sciences and philosophy does not justify us in thinking this or that, as if in unison, this or that; it merely points up our incapacity to undertake a veritable *critique* of the anthropological illusion.

And yet, the model for just such a critique was given to us more than fifty years ago. The Nietzschian enterprise can be understood as at last bringing that proliferation of the questioning of man to an end. For is not the death of God in effect manifested in a doubly murderous gesture which, by putting an end to the absolute, is at the same time the cause of the death of man himself? For man, in his finitude, is not distinguishable from the infinite of which he is both the negation and the harbinger; it is in the death of man that the death of God is realized. Is it not possible to conceive of a critique of finitude which would be as liberating with regard to man as it would be with regard to the infinite, and which would show that finitude is not an end but rather that camber and knot in time when the end is in fact a beginning?

The trajectory of the question *Was ist der Mensch?* in the field of philosophy reaches its end in the response which both challenges and disarms it: *der Übermensch.*[135]

Roberto Nigro

From Kant's *Anthropology* to the Critique of the Anthropological Question: Foucault's *Introduction* in Context

In a short note in the "*Notice historique*" which introduces his translation of Kant's *Anthropologie in pragmatischer Hinsicht*, Foucault tells
us that he envisages devoting a further work to the relationship
between critical thinking and anthropological reflection.[1] Foucault
had begun work on the translation of Kant's *Anthropology*—which
was to form the basis of his secondary thesis for the *doctorat ès lettres*—
while in Hamburg in 1960.[2] There, he also began writing what was
supposed to be an introduction to the "genesis and structure of Kant's
Anthropology."[3] On May 20th, 1961, Foucault submitted two theses
to the University of Paris, Sorbonne: his principal thesis, *Folie et
déraison. Histoire de la folie à l'âge classique* (*Madness and Civilization.
A History of Insanity in the Age of Reason*) supervised by Georges Canguilhem, and his secondary thesis *Kant: Anthropology. Introduction,
Translation and Notes*, supervised by Jean Hyppolite.[4]

For his doctoral work on Kant, Foucault had therefore chosen
to be supervised by one of the leading figures of Hegelianism in
post-war France: Hyppolite's major works—the translation of
Hegel's *Phenomenology of Spirit* into French, his commentary, and
Logic and Existence (1953)—coincided with an upsurge of interest
in Hegel following World War II.[5] Foucault had known Hyppolite

for a long time: in 1945–1946 he had attended Hyppolite's philosophy class at the Lycée Henri IV in Paris; in 1949, at the Sorbonne, Hyppolite supervised Foucault's *Diplôme d'Études Superieures* in philosophy, which focused on "La constitution d'un transcendantal historique dans la *Phénoménologie de l'esprit* de Hegel.[6] Their paths crossed again at the *École Normale Supérieure*, while Foucault was preparing his doctoral thesis. After Hyppolite's death in 1968, Foucault took over his post at the *Collège de France*. In a speech given in tribute to Hyppolite at the *École Normale Supérieure* in January 1969, Foucault remarked: "*Khâgne* students from immediately after the war remember M. Hyppolite's course on *Phenomenology of Spirit*: in this voice that kept on stopping, as if meditating was part of its rhythm, we heard not just the voice of a teacher, but also something of Hegel's voice and, perhaps, even the voice of philosophy itself."[7] In his inaugural lecture delivered at the *Collège de France* in 1970, Foucault affirmed: "I think I am greatly indebted to Jean Hyppolite. I know that, in many people's eyes, his work is under the reign of Hegel, and that our age, whether through logic or epistemology, whether through Marx or through Nietzsche, is attempting to flee Hegel [...] But truly to escape Hegel involves an exact appreciation of the price we have to pay to detach ourselves from him."[8]

Hyppolite must have already been aware, from 1961 on, that Foucault was embarking on a path that would lead him away from Hegel. During Foucault's thesis defense, he noted, with regard to the secondary thesis, that the "historical introduction" to a book on the subject of anthropology is "more inspired by Nietzsche than it is by Kant." The evaluation of Foucault's work did not stop there. In the official report, which gives a summary of the defense, Henri Gouhier, the chair of the jury, made the following remarks: "translation correct but insufficiently subtle. The ideas were seductive but were rapidly developed on the basis of just a few facts: M. Foucault is more philosopher than exegete or historian. The two judges of the minor thesis concluded that it juxtaposes two pieces of work: 1) a historical introduction that is the outline for a book on anthropology and, as M. Hyppolite remarked, one inspired more by Nietzsche than Kant. 2) the translation of Kant's text, which now serves only as a pretext, should be revised. M. de Gandillac advised the candidate that he should separate the two pieces, giving the introduction its full scope as a book in its own right and publishing separately a truly critical edition of Kant's text."[9]

In December 1964, Immanuel Kant's *Anthropologie du point de vue pragmatique*, translated by Michel Foucault, was published by Vrin.[10] However, of the 128 typed pages of introduction to the text, Foucault would publish only six—in the form of the historical note.[11] The other pages, published here in a language other than the one in which they were originally written, would be put to one side, and held in the Bibliothèque de la Sorbonne.[12]

Although known by a very small circle of Foucault's readers, this text has remained unpublished and has long aroused curiosity: some believe that it contains evidence of Foucault's interest in "the positions Kant takes in the [first part of the book] on the difficult question of madness and which type of man is the madman" (when Foucault was working on the *Anthropology*, he was also preoccupied by the distinction between madness and insanity); others are surprised by the way he skirted the debate with Kant around the risk of madness in *Madness and Civilization*—a fudging or absence all the more incomprehensible given Foucault's in-depth knowledge of Kant's *Anthropologie*.[13] Others still consider the Introduction to the *Anthropology* a confirmation of Foucault's life-long relationship with Kant—the traces of which, in this view, are evident in the very last works.[14]

It is tempting to see the introduction as the *truly primitive form* of Foucauldian thought, the source of all the major concerns manifested in his work. We should not, however, give in to this temptation too easily. For these ideas took unforeseen directions and resonated with each other in different ways. Consider, for example, the question of a *pragmatic* knowledge of man as a citizen of the world—a fundamental question which keeps recurring as a leitmotif throughout his interpretation of Kant's *Anthropology*, and will be problematized differently in his later thought. I am thinking here of an interview that Foucault gave in 1984 on "the concern of the self as a practice of freedom,"[15] in which he asks: "How can we practice freedom?" Foucault sees ethics as a practice of freedom, engaged with a freedom that is, in turn, the ontological condition of ethics. These analyses involve the notion of *governmentality*, so important to Foucault from 1978 on, which enables him to focus on the freedom of the subject and on its relationship to others without resorting to a juridical conception of the subject. The practices of freedom thus operate within a *play* of strategic relations, caught in a constant vacillation between the techniques of government (in the double sense of techniques of the self and of the governing of others) and the states of domination, without an originary or grounding level of freedom ever being defined.[16] We see here how an early topic finds its echo in the very last analyses; also the extent to which the context in which it takes on its new meaning has dramatically evolved.

Throughout his life, Foucault kept asking questions which have their source in Kant's work,[17] whether he refers directly or indirectly to it. It is worth noting that, in an entry on his own work written in the 1980s for the *Dictionnaire des philosophes*,[18] Foucault has no hesitation in inscribing his work within a *critical* tradition inaugurated by Kant.[19] But, as Gilles Deleuze argues, if there is a neo-Kantism evident in Foucault's work, both differ in essential ways—especially in their conception of the conditions of possibility. For Foucault, they rely on real experience and not on possible experience, as they do for Kant.[20]

As a number of contemporary studies have shown, there are many issues involved in reading Foucault's works in relation to Kant's oeuvre *today*.[21] In what follows, I merely attempt to understand what was at stake in Foucault's encounter with Kant's *Anthropologie* in the early 1960s. To my knowledge, there are only a small number of critical works dealing with Foucault's short *Introduction*.[22] No doubt the commentary which engages the most directly and systematically with the unpublished text is Béatrice Han's.[23] Han interprets Foucault's text as an attempt to provide a new, subjectless version of the transcendental by denouncing the "phenomenological solution."[24] The problem Foucault faces, then, is how to transpose the conditions of the possibility of knowledge into a nonanthropological domain.'[25] Foucault's *Introduction* makes for essential reading in the sense that it sheds light on the relevance of those themes developed in the last chapters of *The Order of Things*. Han argues that they only refer to the transcendental in general and, it seems, rather undecided terms.[26]

There are two ways of accessing Foucault's text. If we read the text straight through, from the first page to the last, then we are immediately caught up in the twists and turns of an investigation which ranges over the whole of the Kantian oeuvre in its attempt to define the nature of the relationship between the *Critique* and the *Anthropology*, and to understand the role that the question "What is man?" played in Kant's thinking. As Foucault makes clear, one would have to rigorously research the twenty-five years Kant spent lecturing in anthropology while elaborating his critical philosophy, so as to bring to light all the difficulties and risks that the anthropological project implies. Only then would it be possible to see how and to what extent post-Kantian thought managed to forget Kant's teaching on the anthropological question.

But there is another point of entry: one that is indicated in the very last pages of the text; where the question of anthropology is suddenly inscribed within the force field of contemporary philosophy.

Foucault's text should be understood as part of the new climate of intellectual inquiry characterised at the time by the works of Lacan, Lévi-Strauss, Althusser, Derrida, Deleuze, Canguilhem, Barthes, Robbe-Grillet, Benveniste, to name only a few. Nor should we forget that the works which were to have a major impact on those contemporary debates were all published within a few years of each other: from Heidegger's *Nietzsche* to Merleau-Ponty's *Signes*, from Sartre's *Critique of Dialectical Reason* to Koyré's *Newtonian Studies* via Vernant's *Greek Myth and Thought*.[27] This is the *Kampfplatz* Foucault had to deal with: at the heart of the preoccupations of contemporary philosophy he attempted a *true critique* of the *illusions* and the *misunderstandings* in which contemporary thought had become entangled. This was all the more urgent because it opened up the possibility of undertaking a true critique—and archaeology—of the human sciences.

In his *Introduction*, Foucault shows that although Kant's *Anthropology* appears to gravitate around the critical project, it is also orientated by the many anthropological researches that were being carried out in the second half of the eighteenth century, above all in Germany. It is Foucault's aim to uncover the meaning of the emerging field of empirical knowledge which claimed to constitute a new science: anthropology. And he shows that the particular feature of this new domain is this: not only is it the science of man, it is also the science of that which founds and limits man's knowledge. The object of anthropology is neither the human animal, nor is it self-awareness; rather, it is interested in man's natural being, as well as the law of his possibilities and the a priori limitations of his knowledge. On the one hand, then, anthropology concerns man as a natural being, his animalistic determinations; and, on the other, it constitutes the knowledge of man's knowledge of himself, and so involves man interrogating himself, investigating his own limits. The upshot of this inflection of anthropology, says Foucault, is that the shadow of "a classical philosophy henceforth deprived of God" is cast over "the philosophy of our time."[28]

It is this shadow cast over contemporary philosophy that certain philosophical discourses of the 1960s repeatedly sought to critique and to problematize. The most important for Foucault's thinking was the work that Althusser was engaged in at the time. One could even argue that Foucault and Althusser engaged in a play of mutual influence throughout their lives.[29] Consider, for instance, Althusser's discussion of Marx's theoretical antihumanism, or his analysis of Feuerbach, where he makes clear that Feuerbach's attempt to resolve the problems of German idealism by *going beyond Kant and overturning Hegel* ends up as an anthropology; a kind of reflection in which man takes the place of God, in Max Stirner's words.[30] The intellectual climate of the *École Normale*, where Althusser began teaching philosophy in 1948, must have played a decisive role on Foucault's intellectual trajectory. Indeed, it was there that he first engaged with the question of anthropology.[31]

For Foucault, Kant's attempt to think an anthropology raises a fundamental question: Can one have empirical knowledge of finitude?[32] Or, put differently, can one conceive of a sufficiently liberated and grounded knowledge of finitude that would allow for thinking finitude in itself—that is, in a positive form? What, Foucault asks, authorises the conception of anthropology as a positive field which founds all the other human sciences? In this problematization of finitude we find knotted together all the possible threads of a critique of the anthropological question. Now, we should note that by taking Kant's oeuvre as the starting point of this reflection on finitude, Foucault was touching on an essential point that was not neglected by another, hugely influential, interpretation and problematization of Kant's work: Martin Heidegger's *Kant and the Problem of Metaphysics* was written in 1929, but was not translated into French until 1953.[33] Foucault makes no reference to Heidegger in the *Introduction*, but no doubt his text had a considerable influence on him. Not in the generic sense of an influence which stems from his detailed reading of Heidegger from the 1950s on; rather, in the sense that his commentary reformulates a number of questions that Heidegger asks, reversing their presuppositions, and thus calling Heidegger's own interpretation of Kant into question.[34]

For Heidegger, too, was interested in the relationship between critique and anthropology in Kant. His book, dedicated to the memory of Max Scheler (whose anthropology would always remain problematic in Heidegger's view), is an important moment in the twentieth century German endeavour to define a new phase in anthropological questioning. From the opening pages, we see that his analysis turns on the relationship between the metaphysical foundation and the problem of finitude. For Heidegger, the foundations of metaphysics in Kant presuppose an interrogation of man, an anthropology.[35] Hence, in his view, the fourth question of the *Logic*—*What is man?*—where the problem of human finitude arises, only indicates a path, in Kant's philosophy, to the three critical questions toward anthropology. According to Heidegger, the metaphysical foundation of Kant rests upon the necessary connection between anthropology and metaphysics. Metaphysics, therefore, has to be grounded in an analytic of finitude. But Heidegger also underscores the fact that the anthropology Kant presents does not satisfy the demands of the transcendental problematic—it is not a pure anthropology. But this does not prevent Heidegger from pursuing, beyond Kant, his investigation into the transcendental definition of *Dasein*, that is, the foundation of metaphysics as an ontological foundation, taking human finitude as his starting point. Heidegger knew that this would be an ambiguous and impossible task. But it would take Heidegger's move beyond metaphysics for that ambiguity to assume its full proportions and meaning.[36]

For his part, Foucault insists on the vacillations of Kant's analyses, on the difficulty Kant encounters in situating the place of anthropology in the space left behind by an absent God. To be sure, Kant's attempt to define anthropology is not without its ambiguities. But what Foucault wants to highlight is Kant's attempt to show how the empirical character of the anthropology cannot be grounded in itself. On the one hand, Kant's *Anthropology* is subject to the *Critique*—it is restricted to the a priori conditions of knowledge. It is therefore the *Critique* that sets the conditions and determines the field of experience to which anthropological knowledge is subject. Foucault writes: "How to think, analyse, justify, and ground finitude in a thinking which does not take the path of an ontology of the infinite and does not find its justification in a philosophy of the absolute? The question is effectively at work in the *Anthropology* but, because it cannot be thought for itself in the context of an empirical enquiry, it cannot assume its true dimensions there."[37] So, in the economy of Kantian discourse, anthropology acquires its rational order in the sense that it orbits the *Critique*.

On the other hand, Foucault shows that the *Anthropology* works as a transitional moment between critical and transcendental philosophy.[38] What is important to grasp here is that Kant's teaching sets out to demonstrate the impossibility, or at least the great difficulty involved in grounding finitude in itself. At the heart of Kantian thought, anthropology hollows out the problem of the limit that is inscribed in the empirically observed nature of man. When we speak of man, or knowledge of man, we are referring to a layer of knowledge concerned with imperfections, limitations, and failings; in short, with negativity in nature. And it is in relation to this that Kant's teaching appears to have been forgotten.[39]

The web of misunderstandings and illusions in which contemporary thought is caught stems from its failure to register that anthropology only speaks the language of the limit and of negativity. Because of this, it cannot be made it into a positive field that would serve as the basis for the human sciences. Trying to give the *Anthropology* the positive value of a *Critique* is part of the contemporary illusion. Failing to recognise the particular nature of the language it speaks, Foucault argues, the nature of finitude itself has been forgotten. Hence his refusal of all anthropological investigation that defines its origins and its scope by first reflecting upon man in an anthropological fashion. For this is to forget that finitude is inscribed in the relationship between the structure of truth, the phenomenon and experience, and that the analysis of it is bound up with a preliminary critique of knowledge. Having forgotten this teaching, contemporary philosophy could then essentialize finitude, give it the form of a human essence; henceforth, finitude would become the truth of truth. In the end, Foucault argues, anthropology wants to link man's experience to philosophy in a movement in which man presents his truth as the soul of truth. And it is this movement that Nietzsche brings to a conclusion when he shows that the death of God implies the death of man; that the death of God signals the end of metaphysics, and that the place it leaves empty is absolutely not man's for the taking.[40]

This is the direction in which Foucault is going at the beginning of the 1960s. However, his enterprise takes on the form of a combat that would remain incomprehensible if it were not targeting the immense all-encompassing resources of Hegelian thinking. Against the forms of Hegelianism, Foucault musters all the figures which have disrupted the system: Nietzsche, Artaud, Bataille, Roussel, Blanchot, Klossowski, to give just a few names. In a text written in tribute to Georges Bataille, published in 1963 (he worked on it from time to time as he corrected the proofs of his translation of the *Anthropologie*)[41] Foucault affirms that Kant himself closed down the possibilities he had opened up in Western philosophy (which consisted in the articulation of metaphysical discourse and reflection on the limits of reason) when he related, *in the final analysis*, the whole of the critical investigation to the anthropological question. It was replacing the questioning of the human being and the limit with the play of contradiction and of totality that gave rise to this slumber— a mixture of dialectic and anthropology—from which only the hammer of the philosopher would awaken us.[42]

It would, however, be wrong to presume that Foucault was working in this direction from the outset, or that the trajectory of his thinking was unswerving. In this respect, it is worth briefly considering his earliest works. Foucault's first published writings appeared in 1954: *Maladie mentale et personnalité* (which appears to have been written, at Althusser's request, at the end of 1952)[43] and an introduction to Ludwig Binswanger's *Traum und Existenz*.[44] *Maladie mentale et personnalité* rests on a form of realist epistemology which relates to the idea that a pathological fact has a specific content and that man has a concrete and effective truth.[45] Foucault's introduction to *Traum und Existenz*, however, is differently inflected. To be sure, here it is still a question of developing a way of thinking about and of acquiring a knowledge of man. But the manner of proceeding moves from phenomenology in the direction of anthropology. In this text, it is a question of challenging all those forms of positivism that refer to a notion of *homo natura* so as to resituate the question in the context of an ontological reflection which takes existence, the *Dasein*, as its dominant theme—the transcendental structure of which, on the basis also of the echo of Heidegger's commentary on Kant, cannot but send us back to the man-being, the *Menschsein*.[46]

Now Foucault's analyses undergo a major shift in 1957, when the notion of negativity emerges in his work, and takes the place of contradiction. It is the emergence of this notion which will redirect the analysis toward that of *Madness and Civilization*.[47] On the one hand, the reference to negativity seems to be fundamental to our understanding of the mechanism of the constitution of the human sciences (which is one of the major stakes in Foucault's critique, both in his commentary on Kant and later in his project to undertake an archaeology of the human sciences, as in *The Order of Things*). It was only by overturning and transforming negativity into an originary positivity, that of *homo natura*, that the human sciences could materialize: the objectification of madness being the condition of a "scientific" knowledge of man (*Madness and Civilization*);[48] the integration of death being the condition of a "positive" medicine (*The Birth of Clinic*);[49] the manifestation of an "analytic of finitude" being the founding condition on the basis of which "man" could be constituted as an object of possible knowledge (*The Order of Things*).[50] On the other hand, negativity will map out the essential terrain in which limit-experiences can burst forth in their fundamental form. This is what, on the basis of the anthropological circle, *Madness and Civilization* sketches out—in a dimension which, with what it owes to the Nietzschian dimensions of tragedy, does not play any less of a significant role in the combat against the Hegelian *Logos*. Thus, all of these problematizations knot together in an anti-Hegelian combat the model for which was given to us more than one-hundred years ago.[51]

We are now in a better position to understand Hyppolite's remark on the Nietzschian source of inspiration for this text. Perhaps Nietzsche's doubly murderous gesture was all the more radical for Foucault in the sense that it revealed a new direction for his own thinking. Perhaps here too lies one of the keys to understanding why this text remained unpublished for so long: the trajectory of the Kantian question in the field of Foucauldian reflection comes to an end in the historical and genealogical research in which it is challenged and disarmed.[52]

Notes

I have used the following abbreviations when referring to principal works:

AA   Immanuel Kant, *Gesammelte Schriften*
Anthropology Immanuel Kant, *Anthropology from a Pragmatic Point of View*

The information I provide in square brackets and editorial notes is not meant to provide the reader with supplemental interpretations of Kant's philosophy. I have limited my task to indicating those works which can better situate Foucault's reading of it. Nor was it my intention to give the reader general guidance with regard to Foucault's oeuvre. Some of these aspects are taken into account in my afterword at the end of the volume.

— Roberto Nigro

Introduction

1. M. Foucault, *Dits et écrits*, vol. 4., Paris, Gallimard, 1994, n° 348.

2. Kant, *Anthropologie du point de vue pragmatique*, translated into French by Michel Foucault (Paris: Vrin, 1964), reprinted in 1970 and as a paperback in 1991, 1994, 2002.

3. The references "Ak" are indicated in the margin of his translation.

4. Nietzsche, *Beyond Good and Evil*, translated by R. J. Hollingdale (London and New York: Penguin, 2003), § 210, p. 141.

5. Foucault, "Dream, Imagination, and Existence," in M. Foucault and L. Binswanger, *Dream and Existence* (edited by K. Hoeller and translated by Forrest Williams), Atlantic Highlands, NJ: Humanities Press, 1993, pp. 29-78.

6. Michel Foucault, *The Order of Things: An Archaeology of the Human Sciences*, London and New York: Routledge, 2002, p. 270.

Note on the text and translation

1. Immanuel Kant, *Gesammelte Schriften*, vols. 1–22, edited by Preussische Akademie der Wissenschaften; vol. 23, edited by Deutsche Akademie der Wissenschaften zu Berlin; from vol. 24, edited by Akademie der Wissenschaften zu Göttingen (Berlin: Walter de Gruyter, 1907–) (*AA*). Immanuel Kant, *Immanuel Kants Werke*, edited by Ernst Cassirer, Berlin, B. Cassirer, 1912–1921).

2. Immanuel Kant, *Anthropologie du point de vue pragmatique*, translated by Michel Foucault, Paris, Vrin, 1964.

3. Immanuel Kant, *Anthropology from a Pragmatic Point of View*, translated and edited by Robert B. Louden, with an introduction by Manfred Kuehn, Cambridge, Cambridge University Press, 2006. See Louden's 'Note on the text and translation,' pp. xxxvi–xxxix.

4. See the official report of the defense in Didier Eribon, *Michel Foucault*, translated by Betsy Wing, Harvard University Press, Cambridge, MA, 1991, pp. 113-5.

Introduction to Kant's *Anthropology*

1. See vol. 25, 1 and 2 of *Kants Gesammelte Schriften*, edited by Reinhard Brandt and Werner Stark, Berlin, 1997, which contain transcripts of the notes taken by students and auditors during Kant's lifetime. See also Werner Stark, "Historical Notes and Interpretative Questions" in *Essays on Kant's Anthropology*, ed. Brian Jacobs and Patrick Kain (Cambridge: Cambridge University Press, 2003), pp. 15–37.

2. "On Intellectual Pleasure and Unpleasure." See Starke's introduction (*Vorrede*) to *Immanuel Kants Anweisung zur Menschen und Weltkenntniss, in* Friedrich Christian Starke (ed.), *Immanuel Kants Menschenkunde*, op. cit., p. VIII.

3. Ibid., p. VII.

4. With very slight modifications, the preceding pages, up until this point, were published by Foucault as a "Historical Notice" to his translation of Kant's *Anthropology*. See M. Foucault, "Notice historique," in E. Kant, *Anthropologie du point de vue pragmatique*, op. cit., pp. 7–8. The further passages included in the "Notice" are indicated in notes below.

5. Paragraphs (a) and (b) were published by Foucault with modifications in the Vrin edition, op. cit., p. 8.

6. Alexander Gottlieb Baumgarten (1714–1762) gained a certain notoriety for his *Metaphysica*, an exposition of Leibnitzian philosophy. In his course on anthropology, Kant used the chapter on *Psychologia Empirica* (§§ 504–699) from Baumgarten's 1739 *Metaphysica* ("*M*"). See above, p. 110 fn. and below, p. 149: fn 124.

7. In Foucault's manuscript: *Versuch emier.*

8. The pages from this point on were included in Foucault's "Notice historique" in the Vrin edition, op. cit., pp. 8–10.

9. Christoph Wilhelm Hufeland, *Makrobiotik oder die Kunst das menschliche Leben zu verlängern*, Iéna, Akademische Buchhandlung, 1797; Frankfurt am Main/Leipzig, Insel.Verlag, 1995—(Mit e. Brief Immanuel Kants an d. Autor sowie e. Nachw. von Rolf Brück, Frankfurt am Main/ Leipzig, Insel.Verlag, 1988). See *The Art of Prolonging Life*, [London, J. Bell, 1797], New York, Arno Press, 1979.

10. See *The Conflict of the Faculties* (1798), translated by Mary J. Gregor and Robert Anchor in I. Kant, *Religion and Rational Theology*, edited by Allen W. Wood and George Di Giovanni, Cambridge University Press, 1996, pp. 237–327.

11. Tieftrunk (1760–1837), Professor in Halle, was, from 1792 on, one of Kant's most loyal disciples. He wrote on religion. See, Kant, *Correspondence*, op. cit., p. 517.

12. Johann Friedrich Gensichen (1759–1807), mathematician, was one of Kant's regular dinner companions and the executor of his will. See, *Correspondence*, op. cit. p. 529.

13. *Treatise.*

14. See Kant, *Correspondence*, op. cit., p. 529, fn 6.

15. Missing words in the text. In the Vrin edition (p. 9) these words were added: "n'est pas encore entreprise" ["had not yet begun"].

16. Otto Schöndörffer, high school teacher in Königsberg, and editor of Kant's *Anthropology* in the Cassirer edition, Berlin, 1922.

17. Gottfried Less, 1736–1797, from 1765 to 1791 Professor of theology in Göttingen, one of the protagonists of Enlightened Theology in Germany; Albrecht von Haller, 1708–1777, Swiss physician and poet, and Professor of Medecine in Göttingen.

18. "The conflict of the philosophy faculty with the faculty of medicine. On the power of the mind to master its morbid feelings by sheer resolution." *The Conflict of the Faculties*, op. cit., Part III, pp. 313–327.

19. *AA*, vol. XII, op. cit., p. 148: letter written after March 15, 1797.

20. See "A Letter in Reply to Privy councillor and Professor Hufeland," in *The Conflict of the Faculties*, op. cit, Part III, p. 313.

21. C. W. Hufeland (ed.), *Journal der praktischen Arzneykunde und Wundarzneykunst*, Berlin, Wittich, 1795–1808, (4te Stück, Band V).

22. End of the section published in Vrin edition.

23. *De mundi sensibilis atque intelligibilis forma et principiis* (*On the Form and Principles of the Sensible and the Intelligible World. [Inaugural Dissertation] 1770*, in I.

Kant, *Theoretical philosophy*, 1775–1770, translated and edited by David Walford in collaboration with Ralf Meerbote, Cambridge University Press, Cambridge: 1992, pp. 373–416).

24. *Von den Verschiedenen Racen der Menschen (1775)*, in *AA*, vol. II, p. 427–443.

25. "A jerk is not wise; a fool is not clever."

26. Stupidity. See *Anthropology*, p. 99 and the entire chapter *On the Soul's Weaknesses and Illnesses with Respect to Its Cognitive Faculty*.

27. Silliness, See ibid.

28. There is a mistake in the manuscript; Foucault writes "Jorheit" for Torheit (foolishness). See *Anthropology*, p. 107.

29. Illegible.

30. *den* in the text.

31. The title is incomplete. Pietro Moscati (1739–1824) was a doctor and a Professor at the Universities of Pavia and Milan. See Pietro Moscati, *Delle corporee differenze essenziali che passano fra la struttura de' bruti e la umana, discorso accademico del Dott. Pietro Moscati*, Brescia, Rizzardi, 1771; See I. Kant, *Recension von Moscatis Schrift: Von dem körperlichen wesentlichen Unterschiede zwischen der Struktur der Tiere und Menschen* (1771), in *AA*, vol. II, pp. 421–425. Partially translated in W. Wallace, *Kant*, William Blackwood and Sons, Edinburgh and London, 1908, p. 112.

32. *Von der verchiedenen Racen der Menschen*, in *AA*, vol. 2, pp. 427–444 (translated by Mark Mikkelsen in *The Idea of Race*, edited by R. Bernasconi, Indianapolis, Hackett Publishing Company, 2000). See *Anthropology*, pp. 223–224: *The Character of the Races*.

33. Kant writes: "Such an anthropology, considered as *knowledge of the world*, which must come after our *schooling* [*welche auf die Schule folgen muss*] is actually not yet called *pragmatic*," *Anthropology*, p. 4. See also *Von der verchiedenen Racen der Menschen*, op. cit., p. 443.

34. *Von der verchiedenen Racen der Menschen*, op. cit., p. 443: "*Sondern für das Leben brauchbar werden*" ("but to become useful for life").

35. *Von der verchiedenen Racen der Menschen*, op. cit., p. 443: "in which everyone takes his place."

36. Illegible.

37 "*Cité*" in the text.

38. Jacob Sigismund Beck, 1761–1840, Kant's student in Königsberg, *professor of philosophy* in Halle and Rostock and author of a compendium of Kantian doctrine (*Erläuternde Auszüge aus den kritischen Schriften des Herrn Prof Kant, auf Anrathen desselben*, Riga, 1793).

39. *Beilegung*: "Original attribution." See Kant's letter to Jacob Sigismund Beck, 175 [634] (599), in *Correspondence*, op. cit., pp. 481–482. In his translation, Foucault translates the following passage from the German: "*der Beziehung einer Vorstellung, als Bestimmung des Subjekts, auf ein von ihr unterschiedenes Objekt, dadurch Sie ein Erkenntnisstück wird…*," see *AA*, vol. XI, p. 514 (*Correspondence*, p. 481).

40. Ibid., p. 482.

41. Ibid.

42. *Correspondence*, op. cit., p. 482.

43. See *Correspondence*, op. cit., p. 513.

44. "In the practical awareness we lift ourselves above nature and place ourselves outside her mechanism. This is true even if, as human beings, we are also natural objects…," Correspondence, op. cit., pp. 513–514.

45. See Letter dated July, 12, 1797, in *Correspondence*, op. cit., p. 523.

46. "… in order to produce intuitions," *Anthropology*, p. 27.

47. *Das Erfahrende*: "the experiencing." See Letter from J.S. Beck dated June 20, 1797, *Correspondence*, op. cit., p. 512.

48. Play of thoughts.

49. See the footnotes in *Anthropology*, pp. 30–32.

50. Complex, union, sum total, set, totality,

51. *Anthropology*, p. 31.

52. Christian Gottfried Schütz, 1747–1832, Professor for Poetry and Rhetorics in Halle and Jena and, in collaboration with Wieland, editor of the *Allgemeine Literaturzeitung*.

53. *The Metaphysics of Morals*, in I. Kant, *Practical Philosophy*, translated and edited by Mary J. Gregor; general introduction by Allen Wood, Cambridge University Press, 1996, pp. 353–603.

54. *On Rights to Persons Akin to Rights to Things*, Ibid., p. 426 and ff.

55. See Letter to Christian Gottfried Schütz, dated July 10th, 1797: "You cannot really believe that a man makes an object out of a woman just by engaging in

marital cohabitation with her, and vice versa," in *Correspondence*, op. cit., 195 [761] (724), p. 521, where Kant quotes Schütz.

56. In Latin in the text.

57. Household.

58. "*Cité*" in the text.

59. Foucault translates *Mensch* as "Man" (*Homme*). See also the English version of the *Anthropology* translated by Victor Lyle Dowdell (Southern Illinois University Press, 1978).

60. In German in the text. See *Anthropology*, p. 205.

61. In German in the text. See *Anthropology*, p. 3.

62. Johann Christian Reil (1759–1813), was a Professor at the Universities of Halle and Berlin and a German physician. He edited, in collaboration with Johann Christoph Hoffbauer (1766–1827), the *Beyträge zur Beförderug einer Kurmethode* in two volumes, Halle, Curtsche Buchhandlung, 1808 and 1812.

63. Johann Christian August Heinroth (1773–1843), was a Professor of Physical Medicine at Leipzig. His *Störungen des Seelenlebens* (*Disorders of the Soul*, 1818) and *System der psychisch—gerichtlichen Medizin* (*A System of Physical-Forensic Medicine*, 1825) are considered to be Heinroth's most important works.

64. Hufeland, *The Art of Prolonging Life*, op. cit.

65. "The thought came into my mind." See the Letter from Kant to Hufeland dated April 19th, 1797; the letter has not been translated into English.

66. *Friedensabschluss*: peace seattlement. See *The Conflict of the Faculties*, op. cit., p. 281 and ff.

67. Kant writes: "1. *Kentnis des Menschen als Naturdinges; 2. als sittlichen Wesens*," "1. Knowledge of Man as a Natural Thing; 2. As a Moral Being."

68. Kant writes: "*Weltkentnis ist: 1. Naturkentnis, 2. Menschenkentnis; aber der Mensch hat auch eine Natur.*"

69. See *Anthropology*: "*Noch sind die Ausdrücke: die Welt kennen und die Welt haben in ihrer Bedeutung ziemlich weit auseinander: indem der eine nur das Spiel versteht, dem er zugesehen hat, der Andere aber mitgespielt hat*" ("In addition, the expression 'to know the world' and 'to have the world' are rather far from each other in their meaning, since one only *understands* the play that one has watched, while the other has *participated* in it."), p. 4.

70. Johann Wolfgang von Goethe, *Wilhelm Meister's Apprenticeship*, edited and translated by Eric A. Blackall in cooperation with Victor Lange. Princeton, N.J.: Princeton University Press, 1995.

71. *Mind.*

72. See *The Critique of Pure Reason*, op. cit., p. 691 and ff.: "Empirical psychology must thus be entirely banned from metaphysics. [...] It is thus merely a long-accepted foreigner, to whom one grants refuge for a while until it can establish its own domicili in a complete anthropology." See Ibid., p. 700.

73. See *The Critique of Pure Reason: Transcendental Dialectic*, op. cit., p. 384 and ff.

74. This word is difficult decipher in the manuscript, but it is probably *achèvement*: literally *completion*, or *culmination*.

75. See *The Critique of Pure Reason*, op. cit., p. 627 and ff.

76. Mind.

77. Soul.

78. Spirit, but also mind.

79. Faculty.

80. *Esprit* in the text.

81. "The mind tends to procede still further." This is a silent reference to Malebranche. See Book One: *The Sense*, the first chapter of Malebranche's *The Search after Truth*, edited by Thomas M. Lennon and Paul J. Olscamp, Ohio State University Press, Columbus, 1980, p. 5.

82. *Esprit* in the text.

83. Illusion

84. Appearance.

85. This is the title given in Louden's 2006 English translation; Foucault, however, translates *Menschen* by "Homme" (Man).

86. "To know the inner of the human being from the outer."

87. See "Transcendental Doctrine of Method" in *The Critique of Pure Reason*.

88. See "Transcendental Doctrine of Elements" in *The Critique of Pure Reason*.

89. Kant writes Object and Subject with c.

90. Illegible.

91. Word transcribed by hand in the text. Kant's text reads: "*Es* kann *also nur eine Welt sein…*" (my italics).

92. Whole

93. All, totality.

94. "*eines urteilenden Subjekt*" in the text.

95. *Ganze* in the text.

96. In German, the prefix "Ur.." indicates what is originary, while "Ver.." gives the sense of deviation, of dispersion.

97. Determination, purpose.

98. "This truly popular completeness of knowledge."

99. "Knowledge of the world and of the human being."

100. See *Anthropology*, p. 96: "*Der Einfältige, Unkluge, Dumme, Geck, Thor und Narr unterscheiden sich vom Gestörten nicht blos in Graden...*" ("The simpleton, the imprudent person, the stupid person, the coxcomb, the fool, and the buffoon differ from the mentally deranged not merely in degree...").

101. Acumen.

102. Thoughtless.

103. Deep reflection.

104. *entdecken* (to discover), *entfinden* (probably "*erfinden*": to invent), *etwas ausfindig machen* (to descry, to detect), *ersinnen* (to conceive), *ausdenken* (to come up with something), *erdichten* (to fable).

105. "Faculty to provide ideas." See *Anthropology*, p. 143–144.

106. Poetic art.

107. Poetry. See *Anthropology*, p. 144.

108. Rhetoric [Ibid.].

109. Painting of nature. See *Anthropology*, p. 145.

110. Versification [Ibid., p. 146].

111. Conversation.

112. Society.

113. Dinner party (see *Anthropology*, pp. 89 and 179).

114. Sources.

115. Domain.

116. Limit, Boundary.

117. Edmund Husserl (1859–1938), German philosopher, was the principal founder of phenomenology. See *Logical Investigations*, translated by J.N. Findlay, London and New York, Routledge, 2001.

118. See Id. *Cartesian Meditations: An Introduction to Phenomenology*, translated by Dorion Cairns, The Hague, M. Nijhoff, 1960.

119. Friedrich Nietzsche, *Beyond Good and Evil: Prelude to a Philosophy of the Future*, edited by Rolf-Peter Horstmann and Judith Norman, translated by Judith Norman, Cambridge/New York: Cambridge University Press, 2002: "Even the great Chinaman of Königsberg was only a great critic." (§ 210, p. 105).

120. Id., *Twilight of the Idols, or How to Philosophize with a Hammer*, in *The Anti-Christ, Ecce Homo, Twilight of the Idols*, edited by Aaron Ridley, translated by Judith Norman, Cambridge University Press, Cambridge, 2005, pp. 153–229.

121. Id., *Daybreak: thoughts on the prejudices of morality*, edited by Maudemarie Clark, Brian Leiter; translated by R.J. Hollingdale. Cambridge/ New York: Cambridge University Press, 1997.

122. See above, P. 18.

123. Johannes Nikolaus Tetens (1736–1807), Professor of Physics in Kiel; his work also focused on Philosophy, Psychology and Mathematics. He was an important figure of German Enlightnment. See *Philosophische Versuche über die menschliche Natur und Ihre Entwicklung*, Leipzig, 1772.

124. See Alexander Gottlieb Baumgarten, (*Metaphysica*, Halae; Magdeburgicae: Hemmerde, 1739); *Metaphysik*, Jena: Dietrich Scheglmann Reprints, 2004. See above, p. 21 fn.

125. *Nachlass* is misspelt here as "Nachla." See vol. 25, 1 and 2 of *Kants Gesammelte Schriften*, edited by Reinhard Brandt and Werner Stark, op. cit. (See above, p. 18 and p. 142: fn. 1).

126. Aid.

127. It is Tetens.

128. "as they are known (recognized) through the sentiment of the self."

129. "as existing within the brain as the inner organ of the soul."

130. "as constitution of and changes within the brain."

131. "Feeling of oneself."

132. See John Locke, *An Essay Concerning Human Unerstanding*, edited with an Introduction, Critical Apparatus and Glossary by Peter H. Nidditch , Oxford University Press, Oxford, 1975.

133. Kant, 'Metaphysical Foundations of Natural Science', in *Theoretical Philosophy after 1781*, edited and translated by Henry Allison and Peter Heath, *The Cambridge Edition of the Works of Immanuel Kant*, Cambridge, 2002, pp. 171–269.

134. See, M. Foucault, "A Preface to Transgression," in M. Foucault, *Aesthetics, Method, and Epistemology. Essential Works of Foucault 1954–1984*, The New Press, New York 1998, vol. II, pp. 69–87.

135. (My italics). See Friedrich Nietzsche, *The Gay Science*, edited by Bernard Williams, Cambridge University Press, Cambridge, 2001: "New battles. [...] God is dead; but given the way people are, there may still for millenia be caves in which they show his shadow." (Book three, § 108, p. 109); "The greatest recent event—that 'God is dead'; that the belief in the Christian God has become unbelievable—is already starting to cast its first shadow over Europe." (Book Five, § 343, p. 199). Id., *Thus spoke Zarathustra: A Book for All and None*, edited by Adrian Del Caro and Robert B. Pippin, translated by Adrian Del Caro, Cambridge and New York, Cambridge University Press, 2006: "*I teach you the Overman*. Human being is something that must be overcome. What have you done to overcome him" ("Zarathustra's Prologue," p. 3). See also Michel Foucault, *The Order of Things. An Archaeology of the Human Sciences*, London, Routledge, 2001, Chapter VIII, § 2, p. 286 and ch. X, § 5, p. 417 and ff.

Afterword: From Kant's *Anthropology* to the Critique of the Anthropological Question: Foucault's *Introduction* in Context

1. See M. Foucault, "Notice historique," in Emmanuel Kant, *Anthropologie du point de vue pragmatique*, translated by Michel Foucault, Paris, Vrin, 1964, 1994, p. 10 fn: "The relationship between critical thinking and anthropological reflection will be studied in a separate work." In Daniel Defert's view, the work Foucault is announcing here is *The Order of Things. An Archaeology of the Human Sciences*, (London, Routledge, 2001), which was published in Paris in 1966. See Daniel Defert, *Chronologie*, in Michel Foucault, *Dits et Écrits (1954–1988)*, voll. I–IV, edited by D. Defert and F. Ewald in collaboration with J. Lagrange, Paris, Gallimard, 1994, vol.1–4, ibid., vol. 1, p. 26.

2. See David Macey, *The Lives of Michel Foucault*, Hutchinson, London, 1993, pp. 88–89.

3. See above, pp. 22–23 and Daniel Defert, *Chronologie*, op. cit., p. 23.

4. See Didier Eribon, *Michel Foucault*, op. cit., p. 113.

5. See Jean Hyppolite, *Logic and existence*, translated by Leonard Lawlor and Amit Sen, Albany: State University of New York Press, 1997 and Id., *Genesis and structure of Hegel's Phenomenology of spirit*, translated by Samuel Cherniak and John Heckman, Evanston: Northwestern University Press, 1974.

6. See Didier Eribon, *Michel Foucault*, op. cit., pp. 15–30.

7. See Foucault, *Dits et écrits*, vol. 1, op. cit., p. 779. See also Didier Eribon, *Michel Foucault*, op. cit., p. 17.

8. See M. Foucault, *L'ordre du discours. Leçon inaugurale au Collège de France prononcée le 2 décembre 1970*, Gallimard, Paris, p. 74 (translated by Rupert Swyer as "The Discourse on Language," appendix in M. Foucault, *The Archaeology of Knowledge*, trans. A. M. Sheridan Smith, New York: Pantheon, 1972, p. 235).

9. See the official report of the defense in Didier Eribon, *Michel Foucault*, op. cit., pp. 113–115.

10. Kant's *Anthropology* had been translated into French once before: Joseph Tissot's version was published by the Editions de Ladrange in 1863. For more bibliographical information, see Alexandra Makowiak, *Anthropologie d'un point de vue pragmatique. De la faculté d'imaginer*, ellipses, Paris, 1999. On Kant's *Anthropology*, see Holly L. Wilson, *Kant's Pragmatic Anthropology. Its origin, Meaning, and Critical Significance*, State University of New York Press, Albany 2006 and Robert Louden, *Introduction to Kant's Anthropology*, op. cit., p. VII–XXXIX.

11. See above, p. 142, fn. 4.

12. A microfiche copy of the thesis is also held in the Bibliothèque Nationale de France and a hard copy in the Foucault archives at the Institut mémoire de l'édition contemporaine (IMEC), Paris. The text was recently published in France: see E. Kant / M. Foucault, *Anthropologie du point de vue pragmatique & Introduction à l'Anthropologie*, Vrin, Paris, 2008.

13. See, for example, Alain Renault, "Présentation," in Kant, *Anthropologie du point de vue pragmatique*, Flammarion, Paris, 1993, p. 34, for the first reading, and Monique David-Ménard, *Le laboratoire de l'oeuvre*, in *Michel Foucault, Lire l'oeuvre*, edited by Luce Giard, Jérôme Millon, Grenoble, 1992, pp. 32–36 for the second.

14. See, for example, Maria Paola Fimiani's analysis of Foucault's *Introduction* in *Foucault et Kant. Critique clinique Éthique*, L'Harmattan, Paris, 1998, pp. 95–115. See also Riccardo R. Terra's reading in "Foucault lecteur de Kant: de l'Anthropologie à l'ontologie du présent," in *L'année 1798. Kant sur l'Anthropologie*, edited by Jean Ferrari, Paris, Vrin, 1997, pp. 59–171, where the author stresses that Foucault's text was inspired entirely by Nietzsche.

15. M. Foucault, "The ethics of the concern of the self as a practice of freedom," in P. Rabinow and N. Rose, eds., *The Essential Foucault*, New York: New Press, 2003, pp. 25–42.

16. One should also note how far this analysis is from Heidegger's fundamental ontology, at least, as it is sketched out in *Being and Time*, § 41: "Dasein's Being as Care"(see M. Heidegger, *Being and Time*, Blackwell publishing, Oxford, 2005, p. 235).

17. Among Foucault's later texts which deal directly with Kant's œuvre, one of the most important for contemporary debates is "What is Enlightenment?" (in P. Rabinow and N. Rose, eds., *The essential Foucault*, op. cit., pp. 43–57) and the lecture delivered at the *Collège de France* on January 5, 1983, "Qu'est-ce que les Lumières?" (published as "What is revolution?" in S. Lotringer, ed., *The Politics of truth*, Semiotext(e), 2007, pp. 83–95). Contemporary debates around the relationship between Foucault and Kant have tended to focus on these later texts, and on the way in which Foucault makes room for Kant within a philosophical tradition that undertakes a critique of what we say, do, and think through a historical ontology of the self. On this, see Franck Fischbach, "Aufklärung et modernité philosophique: Foucault entre Kant et Hegel," in *Lectures de Foucault. Foucault et la philosophie*, vol. 2, edited by Emmanuel Da Silva, ENS editions, Lyon 2003, pp. 115–134. Fischbach's essay interrogates Foucault's reading of *Aufkärung* and of Kant's introduction of a conscious link between philosophy, the critical attitude, and the present. For further of discussions of this relationship which take these later texts as their starting point see also Christopher Norris, "What is Enlightenment?: Kant and Foucault," in *The Cambridge Companion to Foucault*, Cambridge, 1994, Cambridge University Press, pp. 159–196; Jürgen Habermas, "Taking Aim at the Heart of the Present," in *Michel Foucault. Critical Assessments*, edited by Barry Smart, Routledge, London, New York, 1995, vol. VII, pp. 287–290; Hubert L. Dreyfus and Paul Rabinow, "Was ist Mündigkeit?" Habermas und Foucault über "Was ist Aufklärung?," in *Ethos der Moderne. Foucaults Kritik der Aufklärung*, edited by Eva Erdmann, Rainer Forst, Axel Honneth, Campus Verlag, Frankfurt am Main, New York, 1990, pp. 55–69.

18. D. Huisman (ed.), *Dictionnaire des philosophes*, Paris, Presses Universitaires de France, 1984.

19. See "Foucault," in P. Rabinow and N. Rose, eds., *The Essential Foucault*, op. cit., 2003, pp. 1–5.

20. See Gilles Deleuze, *Foucault*, translated and edited by Séan Hand, Minneapolis: University of Minnesota Press, 1988, p. 60.

21. Among them, I limit my reference here to Andrea Hemminger, *Kritik und Geschichte. Foucault—ein Erbe Kants?*, Philo, Berlin, Wien, 2004, and especially to the first chapter, which analyses Foucault's Introduction to Kant's *Anthropology*.

22. Other than the works already mentioned, see Ute Frietsch, *Michel Foucaults Einführung in die Anthropologie Kants*, in *Kants Anthropologie*, edited by Dietmar Kamper, Christoph Wulf, Gunter Gebauer, Akademie Verlag, Berlin 2002, pp. 11–37. See also, in the same volume, a number of important remarks by Ludger Schwarte on the productive force of the imagination, analyzed on the basis of the pragmatic and popular dimension of Kant's *Anthropologie*, as it is exposed in Foucault's commentary (see Id., *Äusserer Sinn—produktive Einbildungskraft in Kants Amthropologie*, pp. 96–115). See also S. Watson, *Kant and Foucault on the Ends of Man*, in *Tijdschrift voor Filosofie*, 47e year, n° 1, March 1985, pp. 71–102.

23. See Béatrice Han, *Foucault's Critical Project: Between the Transcendental and the Historical*, Stanford University Press, Stanford, California 2002, pp. 17–37.

24. Ibid., p. 6.

25. Ibid., p. 36. On this point see also Carine Mercier's critical remarks in *Michel Foucault et la constitution de l'homme moderne*, Doctoral thesis supervised by Francis Wolff, Paris X-Nanterre, April 2007, p. 66.

26. B. Han, *Foucault's Critical Project*, op. cit., p. 20. See also Id., *Foucault and Heidegger on Kant and Finitude*, in *Foucault and Heidegger. Critical Encounters*, edited by Alan Milchman and Alan Rosenberg, University of Minnesota Press, Minneapolis, London, 2003, pp. 127–162.

27. Pierre Macherey explores this context in "Foucault/Roussel/Foucault," introduction to M. Foucault, *Raymond Roussel*, Gallimard, Paris, 1992, pp. iii–vi. See also Etienne Balibar's "Avant Propos," in L. Althusser, *Pour Marx*, La Découverte, Paris, 1996, pp. iii–iv.

28. See Foucault, *Introduction*, here above, p. 117.

29. See M. Foucault, "Interview with Michel Foucault" in J. Faubion, (ed.), *Power*, New York: New Press, 2000, pp. 239–297 and Id., "On the Ways of Writing History," in J. Faubion, (ed.), *Aesthetics, Method and Epistemology*, New York: New Press, 1998, pp. 279–295, where Foucault underlines what distances him from Althusser with regard to his interpretation of the epistemological break and the place of Marx in the historiy of thought. (On this topic, see Id. *The Order of Things. An Archaeology of the Human Sciences*, op. cit., p. 285, where the point of reference is, nevertheless, to Marxism).

30. See Louis Althusser, *For Marx*, Verso, London/New York, 1996. This book, published in 1965, is a collection of texts published elsewhere between 1960 and 1964. See in particular the texts on Feuerbach, on the young Marx, and *Marxism and Humanism*. See also, Id., *The Humanist Controversy* (1967), in *The Humanist Controversy and Other Writings*, ed. by F. Matheron, translated by G. M. Goshgarian, Verso, London/New York, 2003, pp. 221–305. Etienne Balibar's *L'objet d'Althusser*, in *Politique et philosophie dans l'œuvre d'Althusser*, edited by Sylvain Lazarus, PUF, "Pratiques Théoriques," Paris, 1993 is very useful not only for its discussion of the althusserian problematic but also of what is at stake in the debate around the anthropological question in modern French and contemporary thought. See also, by the same author, *Le structuralisme: une destitution du sujet?* in *Revue de Métaphysique et de Morale*, January 1, 2005.

31. In 1953 at the *École Normale*, Foucault gave a seminar on Kant's *Anthropologie* and Freud (see D. Defert, *Chronologie*, op. cit., p. 19) and between 1954–55 a series of lectures on "Problèmes de l'anthropologie," ("anthropological problems." Lectures at the *École Normale* 1954–1955. Transcription made by Jacques Lagrange of his own notes, 66 ff., IMEC, Paris—Fonds-Foucault {FCL2.A03-02}).

32. See Jules Vuillemin's crucial study, *L'héritage kantien et la révolution copernicienne, Fichte, Cohen, Heidegger*, Paris, PUF, 1954; and Id., *Physique et métaphysique kantiennes*, Paris, PUF, 1955. See also Gérard Lebrun, *Kant et la fin de la métaphysique. Essai sur la critique de la faculté de juger*, Paris, A. Colin, 1970.

33. See Martin Heidegger, *Kant and the problem of metaphysics*, translated by Richard Taft, Bloomington: Indiana University Press, 1997.

34. For Foucault's account of his reading of Heidegger see, for example, M. Foucault, "The Return of Morality," in S. Lotringer, ed., *Foucault live (interviews, 1961–1984)*, New York: Semiotext(e), 1996, pp. 465–473.

35. See Martin Heidegger, *Kant and the problem of metaphysics*, op. cit., § 36.

36. See Martin Heidegger, *Débat sur le Kantisme et la Philosophie (Davos, mars 1929) et autres textes de 1929–1931*, Beauchesne, Paris, 1972. For further discussion of this point see Ernst Cassirer, "Kant und das Problem der Metaphysik. Bemerkungen zu Martin Heideggers Kant-Interpretation (1931)," in *Aufsätze und kleine Schriften (1927–1931), Gesammelte Werke Hamburger Ausgabe*, edited by Birgit Recki , Hamburg 2004, vol. 17, p. 221–250. Rita Casale, *L'esperienza Nietzsche di Heidegger tra nichilismo e Seinsfrage*, Bibliopolis, Napoli 2005, in particular pp. 403–408; Henri Birault, *Heidegger et l'expérience de la pensée*, Gallimard, Paris, 1978, for the relationship Kant-Nietzsche in the Heideggerian enterprise. See also Béatrice Han, *Foucault and Heidegger on Kant and Finitude*, op. cit. In this article, Han insists, on the one hand, on the fact that in his *Introduction to Kant's Anthropology* (which is a veritable prehistory of the chapters VII and IX of *The Order of Things*) Foucault demonstrates: "the unfortunate consequences of the merging by the *Anthropology* of the two understandings of finitude (empirical and transcendental)" and, on the other hand, that Heidegger's analysis "converges on the same critique but from another starting point." She asks: "Can Heidegger escape the problem of the recurrence of the empirical in the transcendental by his using of the notion of being in the world and from the shifting towards an ontological perspective?" On the Foucault-Heidegger relationship in *The Order of Things* see also Gérard Lebrun's remarks in *Notes on Phenomenology* in *Les Mots et les Choses*, in *Michel Foucault Philosopher*, edited by Timothy J. Armstrong, New York, Routledge, 1992.

37. Foucault, *Introduction*, here above, p. 116.

38. Ibid., p. 116–117.

39. In his commentary Foucault only cites eighteenth century authors, but makes the point that the list could be much longer, and go beyond that particular period; no doubt he is thinking of a list that would go up to and include some of his contemporaries, among them Maurice Merleau-Ponty, whose *The structure of behavior* (translated by Alden L. Fisher, Boston, Beacon Press,1967) was published in 1942. While Merleau-Ponty might be the obvious target of Foucault's critique, there are

a number of other philosophers whose work needs to be taken into account if we are to understand the wider implications of what is at stake here and the different paths in which anthropological reflection was engaged in the last century. In particular, the German philosophical enterprise, which developed in the twentieth century: thanks to the works of Max Scheler and Helmuth Plessner, the question of a philosophical anthropology is the order of the day. See M. Scheler, *Die Stellung des Menschen im Kosmos* (*Man's Place in Nature*, New York: Farrar, Straus and Giroux, 1981) and H. Plessner, *Die Stufen des Organischen und der Mensch. Einleitung in die philosophische Anthropologie*, both of which were published in 1928. Without wanting to reduce the diversity of these researches to a homogenous trend, but in order to give, nevertheless, an indication of the range of works in question I am also thinking here of the works of Arnold Gehlen (*Der Mensch. Seine Natur und seine Stellung in der Welt*, 1940, English Translation: *Man, His Nature and Place in the World*, New York, Columbia University Press, 1988) and Ernst Cassirer. During his period of exile in Sweden, and then later at Yale, Cassirer gave a number of lectures on philosophical anthropology in 1939–40 and 1944–45 which formed the basis of his *An Essay on Man. An Introduction to a Philosophy of Human Culture* (Meiner, Hamburg 2006), published in New Haven in 1944. The full lectures and drafts were published for the first time at the end of 2005 (see *Vorlesungen und Studien zur philosophischen Anthropologie*, Meiner, Hamburg, 2005). Cassirer's undertaking is all the more important in the sense that it opens onto an analysis of culture as the human disposition par excellence. Hence, anthropology makes a philosophy of culture possible. On this, see Guillaume Le Blanc, *Les créations corporelles. Une lecture de Merleau-Ponty*, in *Methodos* 4 (2004): *Penser le corps*. See aussi Id., *La vie humaine. Anthropologie et biologie chez Georges Canguilhem*, Paris, PUF, 2002 for a discussion of the idea of a biological anthropology to be reconstituted in Georges Canguilhem's philosophy of norms. We would have to pursue these avenues further to see the directions that Foucault's research would take in the following years. See Foucault's important 1966 article on Cassirer's *Philosophie der Aufklärung*, "Cassirer: Une histoire muette," in *Dits et écrits*, op. cit., vol. I, pp. 545–549, where the importance of Cassirer's work on the relationship between modern thought and the Kantian enigma is made clear.

How anthropology was thought in German culture of the time would remain incomprehensible without taking into account the work of Wilhelm Dilthey and its influence. The opposition that Dilthey establishes at the end of the nineteenth century between the sciences of the mind and the sciences of nature is all the more crucial in that it asks the question of the specificity of the human sciences and their foundation. His work *Einleitung in die Geisteswissenschaften* (1883) was published in France in1942. (See Wilhelm Dilthey, *Introduction to the Human Sciences: an Attempt to lay a Foundation for the Study of Society and History*, Detroit, Wayne State University Press, 1988). On the implications of this see also Jürgen Habermas, *Knowledge & Human Interests*, Polity Press, Cambridge 2004, especially chapters 7 and 8.

40. In a text written in 1946 Althusser affirms: "We have all taken to heart these words from A. Malraux: 'At the end of the century, old Nietzsche proclaimed the death of God. It is now up to us to ask ourselves about ourselves, and to ask ourselves whether man might not be dead henceforth.'" Quoted in D. Macey, *The Lives of Michel Foucault*, op. cit., p. 90. With regard to Nietzsche see Gilles Deleuze's crucial remarks in *Foucault*, op. cit, pp. 124–132 and *Nietzsche and Philosophy*, Columbia University Press, New York, 2006. In particular chapter V: *The Overman: against the Dialectic*, p. 147 and ff. There is no need to stress that the place Foucault accords Nietzsche here is very different to the one he occupies in Heidegger.

41. See "A Preface to Transgression," in M. Foucault, *Aesthetics, Method, and Epistemology. Essential Works of Foucault 1954–1984*, op. cit., pp. 69–87.

42. See Jacques Derrida's important reading of the relationship between Bataille and Hegel: "From Restricted to General Economy. An Hegelianism Without Reserve," in *Writing and Difference*, Routledge Classics, London and New York, 2001. See also Foucault, "The Thought of the Outside," in Foucault, *Aesthetics, Method, and Epistemology*, op. cit., pp. 147–169, where he opposes the philosophy of Kant and Hegel to Hölderlin's poetry and Sade's monologue, Hölderlin and Sade being the manifestation of an antidialectical thinking, a "thought of the outside." On this, see also my study of the "Experiences of the Self between Limit, Transgression and the Explosion of the Dialectical System: Foucault as Reader of Bataille and Blanchot," in *Philosophy & Social Criticism*, 31(6), 2005, Sage Publications, London, pp. 623–638.

43. *Maladie mentale et personnalité*, published by *Presses Universitaires de France* in 1954, was reprinted 1962, but in a version that had been considerably reworked in the light of the gains and overturnings in perspective that had occurred in the meantime, and to which *Madness and Civilisation* and the *Introduction to Kant's Anthropology* bear witness. The new version, which was published as *Maladie mentale et psychologie* (*Mental illness and psychology*, translated by Alan Sheridan; foreword by Hubert Dreyfus, Berkeley: University of California Press, 1987), fits in with the new demands of Foucault's thinking and, by a shift in sense already announced in the title (from "personality" to "psychology") reveals the horizon with regard to which the problematic is situated. Pierre Macherey puts it extremely well: "it is no longer a question of studying the real relationship between illness and the personality, but to examine its historical and discursive relationship to a 'psychology,' which delimits the epistemological field within which the concept is thinkable." (See Pierre Macherey, "Aux sources de l'Histoire de la Folie. Une rectification et ses limites," in *Critique*, 471–2, 1986, pp. 753–774, ibid., pp. 757–758).

44. See M. Foucault, "Dream, Imagination, and Existence," in M. Foucault and L. Binswanger, *Dream and Existence*, edited by K. Hoeller, Atlantic Highlands, NJ: Humanities Press, 1993, pp. 29–78.

45. This concrete form critiqued by Althusser, addressing himself to Politzer, whom Foucault appears to have been inspired by in 1954, in a paper delivered at the *École Normale* in 1963: "La place de la psychanalyse dans les sciences humaines," in *Psychanalyse et Sciences Humaines. Deux conférences*, Librairie Générale Française/ IMEC, Paris, 1996, p. 37.

46. The deepest human meanings are grasped in this text in the movement of the dream, because it is in the dream that man's most originary freedom is revealed. For the implications of this analysis with regard to Husserlian phenomenology, see Judith Revel, "Sur l'introduction à Binswanger (1954)," in *Michel Foucault. Lire l'œuvre*, op. cit., pp. 51-56.

47. See M. Foucault., *La recherche scientifique et la psychologie*, in *Dits et écrits*, op. cit., vol. I, pp. 137–158. These issues are discussed in Carine Mercier's *Michel Foucault et la constitution de l'homme moderne*, op. cit., p. 48–54. On this period of Foucault's output see also Frédéric Gros, *Foucault et la folie*, Paris, PUF, 1997.

48. M. Foucault, *History of Madness*, London and New York: Routledge, 2006.

49. See M. Foucault, *The Birth of the Clinic: an Archaeology of Medical Perception*, translated by A. M. Sheridan Smith, New York: Vintage Books, 1994.

50. See *The Order of Things*, op. cit., p. 340 and ff.

51. See M. Foucault, *History of Madness*, op. cit., Part III, Chapter 5 ("The anthropological circle") as well as "Preface to the 1961 edition," ibid., pp. xxvii-xxxvi. See also Jacques Derrida's extremely suggestive "Cogito and the History of Madness," in *Writing and Difference*, London and New York, Routledge, 2001), in which, on the basis of an interpretation of the Cartesian cogito, a number of fundamental themes relating to the relationship reason/unreason are considered and the very possibility of writing a history of madness *itself* is called into question. See also Foucault's response to Derrida, "My Body, This Paper, This Fire, Appendix II of 1972 edition," in M. Foucault, *History of Madness*, op. cit., pp. 550–574.

52. See Foucault's crucial reading of Nietzsche published in 1971: "Nietzsche, Genealogy, History," in *Language, Counter-Memory, Practice, selected essays and interviews*, edited by D. Bouchard, Ithaca, Cornell University Press, 1977.

semiotext(e) | a history of the present

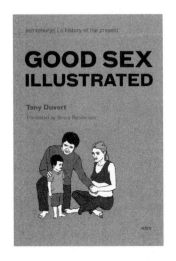

GOOD SEX ILLUSTRATED
Tony Duvert, translated by Bruce Benderson

Written in the wake of May 1968 and Deleuze and Guattari's *Anti-Oedipus*, Tony Duvert's *Good Sex Illustrated* (*Le bon sexe illustré*) was part of the miraculous moment when sexuality could turn the world upside down and reveal social hypocrisy for what it was. Bitterly funny and unabashedly anarchistic, *Good Sex Illustrated* openly declares war on mothers, family, psychoanalysis, morality, and the entire social construct, through a close reading of sex manuals for children. Published in 1973, one year after Duvert won the prestigious Prix Médicis, it proved that accolades had not tempered his scathing wit or his approach to such taboo topics as pedophilia. This translation, by award-winning author Bruce Benderson, will belatedly introduce English-speaking audiences to the most infamous gay writer from France since Jean Gênet first hit the scene in the '40s.

6 x 9 • 184 pages • ISBN: 978-1-58435-043-9 • $14.95

OVEREXPOSED
Sylvère Lotringer
With a new introduction by the author and an additional chapter.

The most perverse perversions are not always those one would expect. Originally conceived as an American update to Foucault's *History of Sexuality*, *Overexposed* is even more outrageous and thought-provoking today than it was twenty years ago when it was first published. Half-way between *Dr. Strangelove* and *Clockwork Orange*, this insider's exposition of cutting-edge cognitive behavioral methods is a hallucinating document on the limits presently assigned to humanity. It also offers a reflection on the overall "obscenity" of contemporary society where everything, and not just sex, is exposed in broad daylight to quickly sink into complete indifference.

"*Overexposed* is an engrossing description of sexual conditioning condoned by the state. A fascinating book."
— William Burroughs

6 x 9 • 192 pages • ISBN: 978-1-58435-045-3 • $14.95

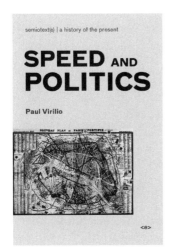

SPEED AND POLITICS
Paul Virilio, translated by Mark Polizzotti
Introduction by Benjamin Bratton

Speed and Politics (1986; first published in France in 1977) is
the matrix of Virilio's entire work. Building on the works of
Morand, Marinetti, and McLuhan, Virilio presents a vision
more radically political than that of any of his French contemporaries: speed as the engine of destruction. It presents a
topological account of the entire history of humanity, honing in
on the technological advances made possible through the mili-
tarization of society. Written at a lightning-fast pace, Virilio's
landmark book is a split-second, overwhelming look at how
humanity's motivity has shaped the way we function today, as
well as a view into what might come of it.
6 x 9 • 176 pages • ISBN: 978-1-58435-040-8 • $14.95

FORGET FOUCAULT
Jean Baudrillard, translated by Nicole Dufresne
Introduction by Sylvère Lotringer

In 1976, Jean Baudrillard sent this essay to the French magazine
Critique, of which Michel Foucault was an editor. Foucault was
asked to reply, but remained silent. *Oublier Foucault* (1977)
made Baudrillard instantly infamous in France. It was a devas-
tating revisitation of Foucault's recent *History of Sexuality* and of
his entire oeuvre. It was also an attack on such philosophers as
Gilles Deleuze and Felix Guattari, who believed that "desire"
could be revolutionary. In Baudrillard's eyes, desire and power
were exchangeable, so desire had no place in Foucault. There is
no better introduction to Baudrillard's polemical approach to
culture than these pages where he dares Foucault to meet the
challenge of his own thought. First published in 1987 in America with a dialogue with Sylvère Lotringer, *Forget Baudrillard*,
this new edition contains a new introduction by Lotringer that
revisits the ideas and impact of this singular book.
6 x 9 • 144 pages • ISBN: 978-1-58435-041-5 • $14.95

ABOUT THE EDITOR

Roberto Nigro is an Assistant Professor specializing in French and German contemporary philosophy. He has studied and taught at the Universities of Bari, Frankfurt, Berlin (FU), Paris X-Nanterre and Paris VIII, Harvard and Basel before joining the Department of Philosophy at Michigan State University. He has published articles on Foucault, Althusser, Marx, Nietzsche and Heidegger, and is currently preparing a book on Foucault.